THE KABBALAH OF ENVY

THE

KABBALAH

OF

ENVY

*Transforming Hatred,
Anger, and Other
Negative Emotions*

RABBI NILTON BONDER

Translated by Julia Michaels

SHAMBHALA
Boston & London
1997

For David Bonder z"l

SHAMBHALA PUBLICATIONS, INC.

HORTICULTURAL HALL

300 MASSACHUSETTS AVENUE

BOSTON, MASSACHUSETTS 02115

http://www.shambhala.com

© 1997 by Nilton Bonder

9 8 7 6 5 4 3 2 1

First Edition
Printed in the United States of America

⊗ This edition is printed on acid-free paper that meets the American
National Standards Institute Z39.48 Standard.

Distributed in the United States by Random House, Inc.,
and in Canada by Random House of Canada Ltd

Library of Congress Cataloging-in-Publication Data

Bonder, Nilton.
[Cabala da inveja.   English]
The kabbalah of envy; transforming hatred, anger,
and other negative emotions / Nilton Bonder.
—1st ed.
p.   cm.
Includes bibliographical references.
ISBN 1-57062-294-9
1. Reconciliation—Religious aspects—Judaism.
2. Interpersonal relations—Religious aspects—Judaism.
3. Ethics, Jewish.
I. Title.
BJ1286.R4B6613   1997   97-7928
296.3'67—dc21   CIP
r97

Contents

CONTENTS

CONTENTS

Introduction

Together with *The Kabbalah of Money* and *The Kabbalah of Food,* * *The Kabbalah of Envy* is part of a trilogy inspired by the Jewish saying: "A person is known in three ways: by his cup, his pocket, and his rage." This reduction of our humanity to three such concrete elements is exceptionally precise about the slice of our souls that it seeks to analyze. The Kabbalah, the Jewish mystical tradition, says we are made of mineral, vegetable, animal, and divine dimensions. The universe of matter and form are mineral expressions; respiration, alimentation, growth, and sex are vegetal essences; locomotion (the search for food, hence the realm of the "cup"), ambition (the realm of the pocket), and competition (that of rage) are animal phenomena.

The eyes that see, the arms that reach, the legs

The Kabbalah of Money: Insights on Livelihood, Business, and All Forms of Economic Behavior (Boston & London: Shambhala Publications, 1996). *The Kabbalah of Food* was published in Portuguese and is forthcoming in English.

that run, the nose that smells, the ears that hear, and all the rest of the human physique derive from this cosmic animal dimension. This is, without a doubt, one of the ways the universe conceives development, and it is the focus of the adage cited above. The animal dimension predominates as an arena for self-knowledge because the borderline between the animal and the divine is the unique territory of what makes us human.

Nevertheless, it is interesting to note that food, money, and sex are often thought of as the most concrete elements of our reality. Thus we can appreciate the wisdom of the adage in its precise exclusion of sex from the animal dimension. Sex is a vegetal element, not to be confused with love. Love, often related to sex, is in fact an expression of competition and shares a cosmic niche with rage. This is why love is part of the animal dimension.

Two questions remain: why approach the negative aspect—rage rather than love—and why translate it as "envy"?

First, the rabbis* recognize that competition comes before cooperation. Both are life movements which are not necessarily differentiated, but appear to be opposites. When we investigate questions relating to rage, we find a universe demarcated by vital spaces: physical, emotional, and spiritual. The interaction of

---

*I broadly refer to "the rabbis" (including commentators cited in the Talmud as well as legendary figures of the Hasidic world) as the keepers of a method of interpretation which understands reality as having multilayered dimensions.

two spaces promotes what we characterize in positive terms as love and in negative terms as rage or hate.

The rabbis dealt with the cup, the pocket, and rage because they were interested in the phenomenon of "obesity," of retention beyond the necessary life-sustaining levels. Life is a process of dynamic equilibrium, and everything that contributes to it is good only in moderation. A healthy diet of food, money, or emotion is one that stays within certain limits.

Only when we perceive the excesses within ourselves, and work to reduce them, does the human soul become visible. We discover more in the effort to return to equilibrium than by staying at equilibrium itself. Thus we know ourselves by our excesses (or our unmet needs) in regard to the cup, the pocket, and rage.

The second issue relates to the title of this book: envy. What is the link between rage and envy? Our interest is the study of excess. Rage is a component of aggressiveness and survival-related disputes, but it is also associated with pain and envy. Hunger, the competition for a mate, and the avoidance of pain are obviously animal characteristics. But what is envy? What is its origin and what is its object?

Envy is the most abstract form of rage. It can store huge amounts of rage, controlling acts, situations, and entire lives. Pouring out vast fortunes of vitality, envy refines deep conflicts and disputes. The fortunes are spent—misused, in fact—without a murmur, though we may protest the stupid waste of huge portions of a country's wealth on weapons. On one level, the Cold War reproduced the conflict of each one of us face to face with the "other," and here is certainly why it became such a personal war for so many people.

The history of the Jews in medieval and modern times is marked by the experience, both individual and communal, of self and other, of "us versus them." Jews are seen as the "other" and have come to internalize that state. The ghettos are the greatest monument to this phenomenon.

Ironically, once this kind of relationship is established, the "I" cannot exist without the "other." This destructive symbiosis is wonderfully described by the famous Yiddish writer Sholom Aleichem:

> A person should always consider the feelings of his neighbors. . . . Thus, if I go to market, for example, and do well there, selling everything at a good profit, and return home with my pockets full of money, my heart throbbing with happiness, I will of course tell my neighbors that I lost everything, to the last kopek, that I am a ruined man. So I would be a happy man and my neighbors would be happy. However, if, on the contrary, I had lost everything at market and came home with nothing but an anguished heart, I would make sure to tell my neighbors that never, since God created markets, had there been such a marvelous one as this. Do you understand? Yes, thus I would be unhappy and my neighbors too, along with me.

The rabbis explain that when people deal with envy and the affective conflicts relating to the other, they are exploring the frontiers of the human being.

For humans, happiness is a more sophisticated emotion than sadness. Tears are more accessible than a guffaw. Strange as this may seem at first, it is easier to empathize with the suffering and failures of others than to offer solidarity in times of success and happiness. At this frontier we catch a glimpse of our real selves.

Thus the last of the Ten Commandments is not merely a corollary of the rest; it is in fact so all-inclusive, so revealing about human beings, that it had to come last: "Do not covet your neighbor's house, nor his wife, his servant, nor his ox, nor anything that is your neighbor's" (Exodus 20:14).

The Rabbi of Radvil explained: "This is the last of the commandments because he who fulfills it will certainly have complied with the rest."

We thus begin a walk through the orchard of envy, of hate, dispute, greed, and generalized conflict—a walk on the unbearable path of the other. This is a passage through the dimension of characteristics we despise in the other because they are so much like our own, of attributes we admire in others that have no place in our lives. This is a fruit orchard in the form of mirrors that reflect us with penetrating brilliance, a journey for which we must be prepared as we face the ghosts of our enemies. These enemies are the guardians of so many of our secrets; much strength is needed to be able, gently, to ask them to hand the secrets over, in order to help us.

The Kabbalah of Envy is a book about the people who inhabit our lives and how they disguise themselves in various ways. It is a book about dissembling friends, enemies, and "others"—and above all, the dissembling "I." It is an attempt to help readers to reread their reality, starting with the redistribution of the lead roles in their carefully self-scripted lives. These scripts are symbolic soap operas of ourselves that determine our destiny, marked as it is by those we accompany and those from whom we flee, as well as by the sorrows and surprises of our journey.

A rabbinical tenet states that he who sees others in the light of himself not only pacifies conflicts, but above all discovers himself. Here is an idea to startle us awake with the suggestion that we find the courage and dignity, when incapable of loving our neighbors as we would love ourselves, to "hate ourselves as we hate our neighbors."

This is a book about the rabbinical discipline needed to widen our range of vision in the worlds of rage.

1

THE STATE OF ENVY

> Human beings feel envy for everyone except their children and disciples.
>
> —*Talmud, Sanhedrin* 105b

Envy is an overwhelming emotion. A person who envies suffers deeply, in a manner conceivable only to other people who share the experience. The face becomes distorted, and deep sorrow takes over the body and installs itself in the throat. This unbearable sensation seems to transcend the borders of even the greatest loss, death itself. As Jewish tradition has it, to be envious is worse than dying:

> Moses, at the end of his life, asked God why he had to die.
>
> "Because I have already named Joshua in your place to lead the Israelites," God responded.

"Let him lead," argued Moses. "I will be his servant."

God concurred, but Joshua didn't like the situation very much. Moses then asked him, "Don't you want me to stay alive?"

Joshua agreed and became leader and master even to him, Moses.

When they went to enter the Holy Tabernacle [where the Ark was kept], a cloud arose. Joshua was allowed into the holy place, while Moses had to remain outside.

Said Moses, "A hundred deaths are preferable to the pain of envy." On that day, he asked to die.　　　　　　　　　　(*Deuteronomy Rabbah* 9.9)

This is a story of great intensity. It shows that envy is often uncontrollable, even when lives are at stake. At first, Moses obviously wants to live at any cost. He finds himself at a stage where he is not theorizing about death, but feels it near. Thus, the comparison of a hundred such afflictions to the sole example of envy has great power. God and Joshua sense that it would not be right to spare Moses, but they cannot face the emotional blackmail of "Don't you want me to live?"

Like a child, Moses is made to feel the bitterness of envy in his own mouth, so that he can understand. And it is certainly not by chance that this dialogue is set as if in the affective world of infancy. After all, Moses' reluctance and later abdication from life characterize the child's world, polarized between "for me" and "not for me," with no form of mediation or sublimation.

"If it's not for me, it's better to die." Moses was reacting to the Joshua who lurks within each one of us, a haunting shadow figure who represents that which we are not. Better to die!

The tragedy of envy is that it usually does not appear only at the end of life, as in this story. Instead, it unfortunately leads to the premature end of many lives. These are the inner lives of people who prefer, like Moses, to extinguish themselves rather than face envy. They wither emotionally from dedicating their lives to avoiding the pain of envy, expending energy to ensure that the "other" will not find success. For such individuals, life itself cannot offer as much pleasure and happiness as the failure of the "other."

The person who envies stands before his own lifeless body, since he is no longer capable of feeling for its own sake. He is a troubled soul, a vampire who feeds not on his own vitality, but on that of others. This behavior is even more frightening because it is not only about the figure of Moses, righteous man and prophet, but about all human beings. We are all envious of everyone—except for our children and disciples. These we perceive as an extension of ourselves, as people through whom we can broaden our own possibilities of pleasure, happiness, and success. Everyone else is a target for envy. Even children or disciples who for some reason are not seen as extensions of their mentors, such as Joshua, cause envy.

Thus, the key question in thinking about envy is how much we narrow or widen the group we think of as children or disciples, and how much this act tends to instill ecological, messianic, or eschatological kinds of reflection.

The universality of envy is effectively demonstrated in a commentary by the great thirteenth-century scholar Naḥmanides, on the phrase "Love your neighbor as yourself" (Leviticus 19:18). He said: "Sometimes we love our neighbor in some situations, and we do him a good turn or a favor. . . . Sometimes we can love him with great intensity, such that we wish him to have riches, property, honor, knowledge, and even wisdom. But we don't wish him to be equal to us, as we always hope in our hearts that we will have more than our neighbor does."

So we see that envy is an endemic emotion, impossible to avoid since it arises in frustrating situations. However, how we each deal with this emotion, how long it stays with us, and the consequences we allow it to trigger all vary a great deal from person to person.

Modern psychoanalysis has brought great understanding of the origins and anomalies of envy. We know, for example, that these go back to a baby's primal moments with frustration and satisfaction. We recognize that it is impossible to avoid the experience of unmet needs, of hunger, cold, pain, and discomfort. At the same time, we are conscious of the need for affection and attention, so that, despite frustrations, we can find equilibrium in the way we live our lives. In this way, we can accept our animal dimension with greater tolerance. This, no doubt, was the century's greatest achievement engendered by psychoanalysis and anthropology. We accept ourselves more, beginning with our animalistic traits; we can analyze ourselves with more compassion and efficacy in regard to our ideals or our divinity.

This book is not so much a study of the pathology of envy as it is a guide to how to live with it. Ancient wisdom, built on past aches and pains, rooted in reflection on the revelation of impulses and attitudes accumulated during our collective history, is an extremely valuable resource in the process of self-knowledge.

To isolate the virus of envy, to identify it amid its innumerable guises, is to invest in the discovery of one's true face, to look at reality from a new point of view. Greater vision in the midst of the darkness of superficiality reduces the aggression of the world and makes our reality more acceptable and more tolerable.

In everyday life, we often consider situations in the light of an objective idea of justice. But in the worlds of rage and envy, an approach from the perspective of injustice is more effective. Above all, injustice has to do with how we perceive a problem or question. To be able to deal with hurt and envy, people often create enormous structures of injustice in their minds and feelings. We must be careful with the rationales we create for our sense of injustice, for they contribute to a waste of time and energy, and to isolation in the loneliness of these feelings. Other individuals or even the cosmos itself may not corroborate these feelings. This also explains why the universe is so indifferent to certain injustices. Some injustices destroy worlds; some ill-perceived injustices can actually multiply the injustice in this world because they are grounded in erroneous assumptions. We will observe this later in greater detail.

For the time being, let us identify some of our best enemies.

Hate as Envy:
Laying Bare the Grudges

> A man with a beautiful wife makes a poor friend.
> —*Yiddish proverb*

The psychoanalyst Melanie Klein, in her book *Envy and Gratitude*, makes important distinctions between the destructive impulses of greed, jealousy, and envy. "Greed," explains Klein, "is an impetuous and insatiable craving exceeding what the subject needs and what the object is able and willing to give. . . . Envy is the angry feeling that another person possesses and enjoys something desirable. . . . Envy implies the subject's relation to one person only. . . . Jealousy is based on envy, but involves a relation to at least two people; it is mainly concerned with love that the subject feels is his due and has been taken away."*

Jealousy means wanting something for ourselves,

---

*Envy and Gratitude and Other Works, 1946–1963 (New York: Free Press, 1975, 1984), p. 181.

unrelated to the person of whom we are jealous. We dream of becoming the object of love or pleasure that we imagine he or she enjoys; once this happens, the individual of whom we are jealous no longer interests us. Jealousy is centered on the self; the other is merely the intermediary for expressing how much we want something.

With envy, however, that something *is* the "other." We are prisoners of someone else. Our desire is the total destruction of the person or thing we blame for not giving us pleasure, the cause of our frustration. We project our frustration onto an individual-object, whose destruction and misfortune come to be a source of pleasure per se. In this projection, we cloud our awareness of the expectation which caused our frustration. And the pleasure promised by envy is never experienced, since envy aims to destroy everything that is not pleasing. Envy is insatiable.

So we see that with both avarice and jealousy, the object sought or needed for pleasure does not become hidden, lost in the avaricious or jealous feeling. With both feelings, the chance to maintain contact with the object that originally sparked them allows us to elaborate strategies to combat them. They are thus more easily neutralized than envy. The latter is more powerful and capable of generating more passionate attitudes. The rabbis characterized the difference between greed (avarice and jealousy) and envy as follows:

> There is a story about two men, one who coveted and one who envied.

The one who coveted was always complaining, "I see how bitter is the work of the Creator. He makes it so that the deserving do not obtain their merit. Why am I poor, while that man, my enemy and neighbor, is rich?"

The one who envied implored, "Eternal One, do not listen to his words and do not allow him to become a prince among your people. Let me die if he becomes rich."

Once an angel appeared to the two men in the desert and called them, saying, "Your prayers and lamentations have been heard. I have come to grant your wishes, and this is what I offer you: you may ask what your hearts desire, and it will immediately be granted. But your wish will also be granted to the other, twofold. This is our accord, and it will not be violated."

The covetous one, dreaming of a twofold wish, said to his neighbor, "You ask first."

The envious one responded, "How can I ask for anything, if at the end you will emerge stronger and richer than I?"

They began to argue until the envious man exclaimed, "God, do unto Your servant the reverse of Your goodness! Blind me in one eye and my enemy in two. Deaden one of my hands and double the measure for my enemy."

Thus it was done, and the two, blind and disabled, remained a pathetic example of shame and disgrace.   (*Berahia ha-Nakdan*)

As absurd as this story appears, we commit similar small acts all the time. Instead of making the most of opportunities and blessings, we prefer the bitterness of a large curse—having our wish linked to what we wish on the other. Still, we realize through this story that, while the covetous man is paralyzed by the situation, the envious one consciously disgraces everyone, including himself. Thus the levels of destruction incurred by avarice/jealousy and envy are quite different.

Envy includes avarice and jealousy. It is a hate that lingers, implacable. Envy is the cornerstone of any grudge. And grudges involve a kind of hate that is preserved unexpended and stored in the form of envious feeling. Speaking of exactly this sentiment, the Bible stipulates, "Do not hate your brother in your heart!" (Leviticus 19:17).

We must be very careful with what penetrates the heart, so as not to pollute it.

Feelings are gates to the external world, where strict "customs control" is necessary. In Jewish practice, customs control is symbolized by the use of strange ritual objects called tefillin. Consisting of two leather boxes containing parchment with biblical texts, the tefillin are tied on the left arm near the heart and on the forehead between the eyes. Using these objects, the person meditates upon waking, becoming aware of the day ahead. He recognizes that a new day is beginning and that those who cannot take a reading of the world beyond routine superficiality will certainly have a more difficult day.

The tefillin are close cousins to the mezuzah, an amulet in the shape of a parchment placed in a small box affixed to the doorways of Jewish homes, kissed on entering or leaving the home. The reason for doing this lies in the opportunity to make the home an internal sacred space. On coming home, Jews touch the mezuzah to remind themselves that everything negative and heavy that may have happened to them should stay outside, or at least be transformed so as to fit into the new environment they are entering. Worries and frustrations should be neutralized by this small object, creating an awareness of what is being allowed inside.

In the same way, leaving home should trigger an awareness of the departure from the space of intimacy and tolerance created there. Thus the street is a place requiring caution, so as not to offend or be misunderstood. In the street, the benefit of doubt, immediate pardon, and freely given love are mere ideals. Until the day when all streets and cities are transformed into a great House, we must be extremely careful to avoid conflict with those whom, in this age, we still call "strangers."

The tefillin are identical in form to the mezuzah exactly because, just like the latter, they are "door amulets": reminders not of a home, but of the absolute home—that is, ourselves. Placed next to the heart and the brain, the tefillin are guardians of these gates. They remind us that the feelings entering and departing the heart must be kept safe, so as not to pollute the world or oneself. At the same time, what penetrates the brain in the form of received or expressed thought must also be fine-tuned, so as to not pollute ourselves or the world with noxious ideas.

The tefillin are thus a warning in starting the day, about the danger of grudges. This is because lasting conflict, envy, and hate fix themselves in the thought-lessness of what enters and leaves our hearts and minds. "Do not allow yourself to hate your neighbor in your heart" is above all an ecological concept.

Envy and Ecology

It's quite common these days to hear about people trying to reflect on the "ecology of the mind and heart." These attempts recognize that a mind or heart can become a storeroom for pollutants that don't disappear over time, that are not degradable. The innate ingenu-ousness of both heart and mind can accumulate so much experiential waste from nonlove, frustration, violence, betrayal, or falsity that our life system cannot process it.

Thus immutable hatreds and conflicts may arise, remaining in their original state, inaccessible to recycling. These are generally hatreds founded on unconscious rationales and structures of logic or emotion. They create reaffirming ideologies or justifications.

"Aren't I right?" we ask ourselves with a certain sly innocence. After all, the human species' survival depends not only on the ability to compete but, above all, on the ability to justify our acts. Justifications, much

THE KABBALAH OF ENVY

more than impulses, are "nondegradable." While impulses may fade away, justifications constantly spur new actions. Every so often, structural housecleaning is needed, by way of crises or shake-ups. Otherwise our minds and hearts become saturated and incapable of producing fertile soil for thoughts and feelings. And disastrous consequences spring from this generalized impoverishment of the quality of thought and feeling, asphyxiated by preconceived ideas.

Many people succumb to pollution and regress to a pure animal state, managing merely to carry out trivial operations of thought and feeling. They are simpletons imprisoned by the idea of "being right," as if this existed in the absolute, a cosmic rightness hidden in some universal records book. They thus confuse divine justice with their own black-and-white vision of the world. They believe that right and wrong are fixed, instead of seeing that rights and wrongs can sometimes invert, with wrongs becoming rights and rights becoming wrongs. They piously worship what is "right" and condemn what is "wrong," when in fact they are idolaters.

This idol worship of the "correct" and the "just" is the ideal habitat for the development of envy.

The first moment in human history when this pollution overflow was dramatically registered is in the story of Cain and Abel. If Cain had killed Abel out of necessity, or even jealousy, the passage would not carry the weight it does. The story is fundamental because it is a tale of envy. The rabbis explain why this is a story of envy, in answering a disciple's question:

God asked Cain why his countenance had fallen (Genesis 4:6). But how, after all, did He expect Cain to react? Why wouldn't his countenance fall when God did not accept his offering?

They answered: "God asked Cain, 'Why is your countenance fallen? Because I did not accept your offering, or because I accepted that of your brother?' "

Desperate, with fallen countenance, not because of one's own failure, but because of another's success— this is the pain of envy.

"I'm dying of envy," we so often say. So as not to kill for envy, one dies (like Moses, as discussed above). Cain had not yet internalized this psychic reversal, which is an important step towards emotional maturity. He opted to kill instead of "dying."

At that moment, the first-ever human seepage of anti-ecological mind and heart occurred. This was the first time that the will to possess supplanted the will to exist. Eradicating the person whose offering is accepted becomes more important than the pleasure of having one's own offering accepted.

In that instant, as the first complete cycle of pollution by "reason" came to a close, the departure from paradise was sealed. The Tree of Knowledge had provided human beings with a psychic structure leading us to crave not the object of our desire, but the elimination of anything blocking the fulfillment of it. We hungered less to *have* access to possession than to *control* that access. Human beings came to want to *have* more than to *be*. Reassuring oneself became more important than feeling secure.

This situation is so very real in cases of unbridled ambition, or even in the small destructive gestures of everyday life. Only if we are hungry is a bird in the hand better than two in the bush. Otherwise, two birds in the bush are better. We have trouble understanding that envy is wanting to appease our psychic hunger with birds in the hand when we aren't truly famished.

Here, then, is the quantum, the smallest unit of envy: preferring the security of having *access* to possession, over the well-being that possession itself can provide. The search for security is insatiable, while the well-being of possession is finite.

Our world's problems with harmony and equilibrium are directly related to this question. Consumer-based societies are, without a doubt, more envious and more desirous of having. They use their energy for being, for the content of their lives, to invest in the acquisition of floor waxers. Each building could have one collective floor waxer, but the wish to have one's own floor waxer is a consequence of the advertising industry's discovery that envy is an intense and powerful human emotion. Even the serpent, to whom the expulsion from paradise is attributed, in addition to being a symbol of envy, is itself moved by envy. Beginning with envy, we mobilize great energy for the destruction of this planet.

Returning to Melanie Klein, we can observe the

implications of envy on the environment. According to
Klein, envy starts with the primal anxiety over the maternal breast. The breast is seen as a "good object,"
while also meting out great cruelty, depriving or not
gratifying the infant with what he or she expects. Envy
originates directly from the destructive impulses regarding the breast. Thus ecological issues are about our
difficulty in dealing with the great breast of Mother
Earth, which sustains us. We love her but we sadisti-
cally attack her breast. So we envy our environment and
for this reason want so much from it, instead of experiencing or feeling what comes from it.

Rabbi Zalman Schachter-Shalomi has expressed
the feeling of envy as a poker-game syndrome. What
happens in this game? Each player tries to hide his
hand from the other. Winning depends on another's
loss, and the pleasure is even greater if the loss is due
to a bluff. Bluffing is the sadistic element, the greatest
cause of ecological imbalance. This is because victory,
overcoming an adversary, and the reward for victory are
nothing compared to the opponent's personal defeat.
Games of this kind expose patterns of noncooperation,
which feed envy and grudges. The pleasure derived
from holding a grudge distorts the instinct for seeking
to be, to enjoy or experience, and sparks the wish to
have. The player comes to play not for the sake of the
game, nor even to win, but to see the other lose. The
fact of another's loss is more pleasurable than winning.

Envy turns human beings into peerless predators.
Not only greed and ambition are at play in the rundown

of natural resources; the ideology of having so that others won't have sets up great discrepancies in the distribution of these resources.

Envy and Idolatry

About the tenth commandment, which says we should not covet others' belongings, the Radviler said: "He who doesn't have the self-discipline to obey this prohibition of coveting should begin anew, starting with the first commandment: to love and recognize divine justice; because if such an individual really believed in God, he would not envy that which was allocated separately as part of the portion of his neighbor."

Envy is the ultimate proof of the civilizing and organizational driving force behind the Ten Commandments. Even the original abstraction of God's existence is put into check when we come face to face with envy at the end of the list of commandments. This is because, in the rabbinical system, envy reveals not only disbelief in the Divine Order, but also the detours that lead to idolatry, for those who think they believe in God. These are, without a doubt, more numerous than the unbelievers, and considerably more destructive to the system.

In truth, a self-professed believer who envies believes in something or in some kind of justice that is not absolute. He most likely has a private god, with a personalized worldview and agenda. His worldly manifestation comes via the confirmation of small victories or personal conquests, which make him arrogant or ego-centric.

Such people speak of their shining "lucky stars." As they move through a sophisticated cosmic schedule of personal success, they rejoice in each purported achievement. Any setbacks are attributed to a mere slip of a God who "writes with crooked lines" but will soon make known a final destiny confirming their expectations of personal victory.

People with such expectations are classical envi-ers. They envy when they don't possess the object of their desire and they envy when they do. In the latter situation, they fear that others may also obtain personal victories. When this happens, they must seek an expla-nation, and this causes great theological difficulty, lead-ing to the pagan belief that others also worship gods of considerable power, that their stars also shine.

The potential for idolatry actually lies within each one of us, in constant conflict with monotheism. After all, the belief in a sole God responsible for all beings, striving to accommodate the largest possible number of personal victories within reality, is complex and con-troversial. It is quite difficult to sell an idea—monotheism—when it challenges the feelings of envy that come so naturally to humans. A God concerned with collective justice does not always attend to a par-ticular individual's personal needs.

Monotheism is still more difficult to fully accept when widened to include not just a specific group, but all groups or even all species. A God who acts justly for

Jews and Christians, Cubans and Americans, spiritual-
ists and rationalists, or for human beings and whales
in extinction, brings out very complex expectations of
reality. The existence of envy is evidence of this difficulty—a *kelippah* (shell), as kabbalistic tradition puts
it.

The decision to accept the notion of one God depends above all on a feeling of gratitude. From time
immemorial, belief in divinity emerged from a deep
feeling of gratitude experienced by humans. Over mil-
lennia, this feeling guaranteed the survival of religious
and spiritual ideas. While envy is a constant witness to
the irrationality of belief in God, gratitude operates in
the opposite direction. Since both are feelings, they will
never prove or disprove each other. Still, envy is indis-
putably a unit of idolatry.

The establishment of a messianic era implies not
an external proof of the truth contained in God, but the
absolute predominance of gratitude. It is a time when
people will no longer identify with envy and will consider it foreign. Combating the world's levels of envy,
we may say with the rabbis' support, is fundamental to
the eradication of idolatry.

2

RANCOR IN OTHER WORLDS

Attempts to establish and rank priorities always underscore the limits of the human mind. But they can at least serve to create an analytic model. Thus we will try to take reality apart in the classical manner suggested by the Kabbalah, based on four dimensions or worlds. These worlds, coexistent and superimposed on one another, serve to transport mundane events, starting with the most concrete, into more subtle dimensions of reality.

Scientists have shown that small quantities of certain substances behave in a particular manner. But when these substances are taken in regular doses, they tend to accumulate and behave differently. Hatred is similar in nature.

Biblical texts and rabbinical interpretations offer

us some classifications of hatred. In Leviticus 19 (the passage known as Kedoshim, "Holiness") we find three different forms of hatred: *lo tisna* (do not hate); *lo tikom* (do not seek revenge); and *lo titor* (do not bear a grudge).

The first, "do not hate," is about the most common form of hatred, reactive hatred. We immediately hate someone who is disagreeable to us or subjects us to suffering. This is a temporary condition, the equivalent of having our foot stepped on. The reaction to the pain is an immediate animal readiness to fight or curse the aggressor. Quickly, however, as the pain and discomfort die down, there is also a reduction in the victim's total contempt for the agent of his suffering. If the aggressor reacts with regret, identifies with the pain, or simply recognizes his error and expresses non-intent, it is possible not only to eliminate the hate, but to end up exchanging courtesies. We will discuss later how this type of hatred, experienced frequently—having one's foot stepped on repeatedly—even given due excuses, ends up creating a certain kind of cumulative hatred. This first level of hatred deflection is described by the traditional Hebrew term *sinat ḥinam* (causeless hatred).

Having one's foot stepped on gets complicated when the aggressor's reaction is not one of identification or anything positive at all. Then, hatred is not temporary and creates two other kinds of deviations: *nekimah* (revenge) and *netirah* (grudge). To explain and differentiate them, the rabbis offer us examples:

Do not seek revenge. How to define "revenge"?
Imagine that one person says to another, "Lend
me your sickle," and the other denies the request.
The next day, the latter says, "Lend me your
chisel," and the former replies that he will not
lend the chisel, as the sickle was not lent to him.
Such behavior is called revenge.

Do not bear a grudge. How to define a
grudge? Imagine that one person says to another,
"Lend me your chisel," and the other refuses.
The next day, the latter says, "Lend me your
sickle," and the first replies, "Here it is. I am not
like you, who would not lend me your chisel."
Such behavior is how grudges begin.   (*Sifra*)

These examples present exceptional teachings
about hatred. First, we find a situation where the focus
is on the individual who reacts to the denial of his request, nothing being said about the person who originally refuses to lend a tool. The medieval commentator
Rashi takes on this question, explaining that we are not
interested in analyzing the act of pettiness, but the hatred which is fed and cultivated in the heart of the one
whose request is frustrated. After all, as we will later
see in the sections "No More Mr. Nice Guy" and "Living with Ill Will," no one is obliged to lend something.

However, a source of great insight lies in the huge
difference between the reactions of the frustrated individual. Clearly, the rabbis were going beyond the definition itself to explore the limits of revenge with greater
precision. In the examples related above, the objects

requested are different. In the first case, there is a typical attitude of revenge: the offended party waits until
the following day to pay back the insult, over a chisel.
In the example of a grudge, the request for a chisel is
avenged with the sickle. Why were the objects different
and why are they inverted in the two cases? The expla-
nation is given in the *Havanat ha-Mikra*:

> The examples of the sickle and the chisel were
> deliberately chosen. This is because the sickle is
> a more delicate object, subject to wear and tear
> during use, requiring constant sharpening. In this
> manner, revenge is truly illustrated, since the
> chisel is a more resistant tool, which hardly gets
> worn down during use. In other words, if the sec-
> ond individual had asked for a chisel, the first
> would not have refused to lend it. His refusal is
> due to the fact that a sickle is a fragile object.
> The reaction of the second individual is thus pure
> vengeance, as he refuses his neighbor a very triv-
> ial item just because an item of great value was
> denied to him.
>
> If we had the inverse situation, where the
> initial denial was about a chisel, followed by a
> refusal to lend a sickle, the example would not be
> one of revenge. This is because the refusal of a
> sickle would be justified: "If you are concerned
> about lending me your chisel, imagine my rea-
> sons to worry about my sickle, which is more
> fragile."
>
> Thus, the term "revenge" applies only to

the retribution of evil in greater measure than that
in which it originated; it does not apply to retribution in equal measure, and certainly not to lesser
evil.

Why is all this so important? Because, in the same
way that people have the right not to lend something,
this right should also be safeguarded for those who ask
to borrow yet won't lend when asked to do so. This in
itself is not revenge. The right not to be a "nice guy" is
not encouraged; it is condoned. (Later we will discuss
the circumstances where this is encouraged.) The limits
of revenge are in retribution; these become evident
when there is no real reason to refuse a loan.

Thus there is a distortion of hatred when one person refuses to lend a sickle and another responds by
denying his chisel. A person who expects another to
freely give his sickle cannot feel true attachment to his
chisel without revealing signs of revenge.

Revenge is thus one way to preserve hatred, the
feeling of being stepped upon, a feeling appeased only
by stepping on the aggressor's foot. But there is a worse
situation: bearing a grudge. While revenge is played
out in the immediate (or near-immediate) discharge of
hatred, grudges prolong hatred.

By reacting with superiority to a request from
someone who has previously denied us something, we
actually manage to deepen a conflict. When a person
concedes a loan with the hatred expressed in the phrase
"I'm not like you," he manifests the wish to seek ven-

geance, later and in another manner. At the same time, the borrower's hatred grows, since he feels admonished both for how he behaves and for who he is. His conflict moves from the level of request-denying to that of being made to feel like an inferior human being. An overall process of hatred sets in as one seeks to punish the other. Over time, the circumstances of the hatred are forgotten, with only the grudge itself remaining.

This superior attitude carries within it a great deal of violence and sets up more sophisticated structures of hatred. It is interesting to note that in the example about grudges, the violent reaction arises over the instrument that brings rancorous superiority: the chisel. Because such a primitive tool should be easily lent and borrowed, the person who asked to borrow it experiences a more painful sensation than that of rejection itself. If he had asked for the sickle, knowing its special value, he might not hate the person who refused him so much.

The example illustrates so very well the depth of the lender's hatred, because as a magnanimous or superior act he is even willing to part with his sickle, a tool that requires greater care. He is thus willing to risk putting a valuable object in the hands of someone he believes hates him, just to show how different the two of them are.

These are situations that belong to the childhood world of nonverbal readings of behavior. Children feel especially hurt by unfairness over issues of lending and borrowing. These are the first experiences of social relations, out of which experiences of hatred can grow into revenge and feuding. Not being lent something that requires no sacrifice by the lender generates potent hatred. Here is why ending a feud depends on an understanding of the real value things have to another individual. This is the only way to neutralize the destructive power of having been denied something that apparently would be "no skin" off someone else's back.

Human Expressions of Rancor in the Four Worlds

Regarding hatred, the rabbis said that there are four types of people:

1. one who is easy to provoke and easy to appease, where the negative is neutralized by the positive;
2. one who is difficult to provoke and also difficult to appease, where the positive is neutralized by the negative;
3. one who is difficult to provoke and easy to appease—this one is a sage; and
4. one who is easy to provoke and difficult to appease—this one is wicked.   (*Pirkei Avot* 5:14)

What we see in these four examples is a classical dissection of behavior, according to Jewish tradition. In my book *The Kabbalah of Money*, we saw a parallel approach: *nothing*, the *fool*, the *wicked*, and the *sage*.

These personalities appear once more in the framework of this book. *Nothing* refers to a person who is totally lost, who is easily provoked, and just as easily appeased. He carries out two tasks, that of getting angry and then having to calm down. In fact, he is a nothing, since he is always creating problems for himself that he can easily solve. His rancor is small, but his loss of time and energy belong to those who are carried, swept along by life. He has little space for growth.

The fool is a person rarely provoked and rarely appeased. This type of individual understands that we should not easily subject ourselves to provocation. He apparently has already internalized a posture allowing few life situations to provoke him. But this is a rational, external posture, since once provoked, he cannot find ways to sublimate the provocation. He is called a *fool* because he only partially understands the necessary effort to remain unaffected. Such is the case of many people who are socially repressed by their upbringing and who become prisoners of their impulses and their ethics. They argue and theorize but cannot live out what they apparently know and believe.

The situations of the wicked and the sage are obvious. The former loses himself in the swamp of rancor, while the latter wanders through the orchard. The wise one has a deep reading of reality which in itself hinders provocation, and also gives him the capacity to quickly adjust to life situations and control himself easily.

The table on page 34 provides a correlation between each of the different levels of rancor and the worlds of the Kabbalah. Physical rancor requires immediacy; hatred is ferociously expressed, but once the discharge is made, balance is achieved and no grudges are formed. Physical rancor is about a more reflexive animal reaction and, when excessive, can create distortions leading to greed. In the human dimension, it represents a *nothing*.

In the mental dimension, vengeance is plotted via rational comparison and self-justification. Hatred is not an immediate reflex, but once a person is hurt or frustrated in this dimension, it is very difficult to appease him. He will find it necessary to hang on to his hatred until he can tame it or pay back the person he identifies as its cause. This, as we saw earlier, is the *fool*, whose rewards are jealousy and pride.

In the affective dimension, we find the symbolic wish to hate someone with whom we quarrel easily, and whom we are always ready to criticize and judge with suspicion and malice. It is difficult to make excuses or stay quiet about any error he commits. We are in the world of envy that overflows into arrogance. We take on the posture of the wicked one and sink into grudges. We feed hatred for long periods, sometimes for a lifetime.

All these previous dimensions are part of the opening of "windows" to another world that is detectable, although it is subtle and difficult to define. It belongs to the level of things that cannot be "captured in a net," that are not patently expressed or provable, even though they reside in everyday life and perceptions. This is the spiritual sphere, where we may find long-

World	Dimension	Expression in Hatred	Human Expression	Expression in Behavior	Expression in Malice
ASIYYAH Action	PHYSICAL	SINAH (hatred)	NOTHING Easily enraged Easily appeased	VORACITY (Greed)	SLANDER (Motzi Shem Ra)
YETZIRAH Formation	EMOTIONAL	NEKIMAH (revenge)	FOOL Hard to enrage Hard to appease	JEALOUSY (Pride)	TALE-BEARING (Rekhilut)
BERIAH Creation	MENTAL	NETIRAH (feud)	WICKED Easily enraged Hard to appease	ENVY (Arrogance)	EVIL TONGUE (Lashon ha-Ra)
ATZILUT Emanation	SPIRITUAL	KARMIC	HERETIC Cannot be appeased	SKEPTICISM	HERESY

established forms of rancor, unlikely to be erased or diminished. In this sphere, we may experience a loss of vitality, the tying up of issues from one generation to the next, or even so-called supernatural situations.

This is about the inexplicable, which can come from very complex levels of subtlety, generating or appearing to generate tormenting consequences. This dimension is created and fed by the other dimensions, but once it exists, it also interferes in the others. Such matters will only find relief with "redeemers" (*goelim*), who can break the cycles feeding these very subtle, karmic hatreds. For the most part, they are set off by obsessive forms of revenge or grudge-bearing. To avoid getting lost in the subtlety which defines it, I will deal with this dimension in greater depth later.

What's important is to discern these different levels and utilize them as models for the situations we will be discussing.

Stealing the Emperor's Clothes: The Temptation of Pride

"As for pride, it is the vestment of the Eternal One" (Psalm 93:1). The Rabbi of Stretyn explains: "The Eternal One covers Himself with a vestment He makes from the pride that wise people are able to abandon."

Pride is one of the most important ways to store rancor. We constantly act under its influence. This is where the justifications for maintaining many of our grudges come from.

Many people believe that humility is the opposite of pride, when in fact it is a point of equilibrium. The opposite of pride is actually lack of self-esteem. A humble person is totally different from a person who cannot recognize and appreciate himself as part of this world's marvels. His attitude is thus different from someone full of pride, totally centered on himself.

Pride induces the belief that we are "right," hindering the ability to compare and contrast situations from different perspectives than one's own preformed opinions or judgments. The pride we are talking about is invisible, a pride that infiltrates our hearts by way of self-esteem, a normal human feeling. The Besht (the Baal Shem Tov) illustrated this well when he said:

> It is so natural for a talented person to be taken over by pride that he rarely is aware of it. Only when he makes the effort to be more humble in his relationships with others does he realize how drunk with pride he was. This is like a man who, traveling in his carriage, falls asleep. The coachman ascends a hill and, once reaching the crest, travels over a long flat stretch. When the traveler awakens and is informed that he is on a hill, he cannot believe it. Only when the descent begins does he realize how high he was.

Many times, talent has nothing to do with it. The Bershider comments: "Building pride needs no foundations. A man can cling to his bed, in his freezing house, wrapped in a mended blanket, and even so feed in his heart the feeling: 'I am the best! I am the best'!''

Of all types of pride, the pride of a person who thinks he is growing as a human being is the worst. Pride in this case is a traitorous trap, because as the person gains a feeling of superiority from his growth, he creates an obstacle to further growth. Rabbi Mendel Libavitzer said, "There is no worse pride than the pride of the pious." Everyone should learn to see through his or her supposed piety. The pride of a pious man is the pride felt by one who sanctifies himself because he does not feel self-centered. The Besht tells this story:

> A learned and charitable man had constant problems with his pride. He was told that if he could learn to be humble, he would become a perfect person. The man listened to the advice and dedicated himself to the study of the question of humility until he knew, almost by heart, all the recommendations to avoid pride. One day, someone failed to show him due deference. The man, who thought himself humble, came to the person and said, "You fool! Don't you realize that since I learned about humility, I am a man of perfect character, deserving respect?"

This is the biggest trap for people trying to invest in personal and spiritual growth. During the process of self-affirmation, so crucial to an awakening, we are systematically tempted by the forces of pride. We come up against this constantly, living as we do in a period of great transition that spurs the preservation of the one nonperishable good: self-knowledge. When institutions and ideologies weaken, we find no space for investing in our lives, except via personal growth. And while for humanity this is an extremely enriching trend, it can also cause regression, because so many people misunderstand personal investment, viewing it as an actual good. They want to *possess* growth as one possesses a diploma, instead of *living* it and enduring the pangs that are an intrinsic part of growth.

As we saw earlier, this is a characteristic of envy, where we try to grow, merely hoping to create capital (that is, respect and influence). This is how the *fool* most often becomes *wicked*, how jealousy becomes envy. At issue is the capacity to find internal happiness, to develop a pleasing relationship with oneself that depends minimally on others' expectations.

Situations of excessive jealousy that become malignant with envy turn apparently healthy people into the slaves of what other people think. They get something in this world, and even before they fully enjoy the pleasure of it for themselves, they are thinking of the delight they will feel on relaying their luck to those they envy. They experience a short-circuit in their capacity to *be*, which is constantly lived out as *having*.

Rooted in different types of needs, personal growth, spirituality, or mere self-esteem can thus become instruments of envy, perhaps even the worst type of envy.

For those who envy, the pride of the pious is the

most sophisticated mask of envy. This is the highest level that can be reached by a person who envies profoundly. He finds an imaginary world of perverse personal theologies, with the one aim of preserving a sense of victory or success, in relation to others. The need to possess, instead of feeling, is so huge that it becomes necessary to personalize and mold the cosmos to one's small reality of unresolved rancors. The pride of the pious is pride's most radical expression. It is a prevalent behavior, often covering up enormous frustrations.

The greater our ability to live an internal life which does not depend on others for the affirmation of "personal victories," the closer we come to being humble. Dependence feeds pride. Humility does not imply lack of self-esteem; on the contrary, tolerance and the ability to empathize are the very consequences of an individual's respect for himself. It is actually a posture reflecting an internal reality, where the awareness of one's own weaknesses generates great esteem for human nature. Hence the rabbinical adage: "Humility removes the fear of enemies, disputes, and pain."

The image of pride which the rabbis drew is an expression from the world of the shadow, the dark side of self-esteem and personal growth. Here is the last bulwark of the shadow world, annulling the light created in the affirmation of self-esteem and the search for growth. Coming on the heels of a great effort to reach the light, pride can be thought of as a negative mathematical sign that cancels all credit acquired in the luminosity. The rabbis spoke of the process this way:

The Maggid, describing the ritual for retiring to sleep, explained: "In preparing for sleep, the disciple of the sages should become accustomed to making an accounting of his deeds and attitudes during the day. And if the heart of a disciple fills up on thinking that he made excellent use of his day, the angels of the seven heavens pack all his good deeds into a ball and throw it into the abyss."

This instant cancellation of all constructive effort is the source of great regression in both individual and collective human development. In the symbolic language of Jewish mysticism, it is represented as a lack of cooperation in the construction of the Divine Garments. Mythically, it means a delay in the preparations for the crowning of a new era where humility will be sovereign. In codes of the unconscious, a metaphorical relationship exists between divinity and cooperation among humans. Humans free themselves of pride, and using this same castoff material, the Eternal One makes His garments.

Humility as Maximum Wisdom

Not everyone is happy with his appearance, but all are happy with their brains!

—Yiddish proverb

In a book entitled *Among Human Beings and Their Likenesses*, the thirteenth-century Spanish com-

mentator Rabbenu Baḥya comes to an interesting conclusion by juxtaposing sacred texts. From the Midrash
he observes the saying "The ankle [i.e., foundation] of
humility is the fear of God" (*Shir ha-Shirim Rabbah*
1:9), and from Proverbs (1:7) he takes, "The fear of
God is the head [i.e., beginning] of wisdom."

According to him, we can infer from the two texts
that humility is superior to wisdom, since "fear of
God," the head or crown of wisdom, is no more than the
ankle of humility.

We should first understand the meaning of the specific concept of "fear of God," which the rabbis refer to
as "fear of Heaven" instead of trying to understand it
in the simple analysis of the words "fear" and "God."
This is religious language, commonly viewed as
churchy and archaic. The popular image of God as
"Someone who hears and sees everything" is a product
of religious pedagogy that most people fail to update
with more sophisticated observations of reality as they
leave childhood behind. But a true lay translation of
this idea would be to say that those who fear God relate
to life through values and notions that transcend the
logic of immediate gain.

Because it expresses extremely subtle feelings and
perceptions, religion comes up against enormous communication difficulties in the transmission of ideas and
concepts. Childish perceptions, by way of examples,
images, and concrete associations that appear to contra-
dict spirituality's subtle essence, are inevitable. And
while on the one hand this is responsible for the tragedy

of multitudes who stand by an infantile idea of religion, on the other it is still the most efficient method available for initiation.

Initiation is the process of "ignition" or activation of the individual's soul. Once ignition has happened, the route taken is a constant search to align perception and reality. Ignition happens by way of the reverence felt for a master, regardless of his or her tradition or religious institution.

Who is the master? The master is the model we trust. Given trust, we seek to understand religious language, offering second, third, or however many chances necessary for understanding. The master is a facilitator of religious communication. The disciple, the person who respects and reveres the master, hears in his words and sees in his attitudes many elements beyond comprehension. But, because he loves and respects the master, he seeks, often over his entire life, the meaning and the reasons behind those words and acts.

This is similar to a child who recognizes its parents' wisdom years after an event. Such revelation of wisdom is only partly due to what is said or done. Much of it is the result of the reverence or love we hold for our parents and the fact that deep inside, we refuse to accept that someone as special as a master could say something trivial or act frivolously. This element of perplexity and intrigue is what will permit us to understand ideas that wouldn't otherwise be of interest or concern. The master is indispensable to the initiation process, since he or she is the key to the absorption of concrete notions that only time and maturity allow us to understand in all their depth and subtlety.

All this is to say that "fear of God" is a concept that is difficult to understand without having known someone who feared God. This is the only way to understand that the term is not about terror, but about having great intimacy with God. A master is not a prisoner of dogmas, but someone who can try a daily praxis, highly influenced or almost totally generated by abstract, subtle principles. And, because he can detach himself from the dimension of the obvious and the commonplace, he sees so much further that he can even observe the obvious and the common from a distance. He has reached wisdom.

For a person to arrive at a "fear of God," he must leave behind the cult of the god of rewards, the god of immediate necessity, the god of power, the god of personal veneration, and manage to eliminate the childish elements of his symbolic perception of God. He must do the same with the word *fear* and cast off the fear of others, the fear of self, and the fear of pain to permit himself to feel fear of only that which it is proper to fear. Only in this way can his fears transform themselves into zeal or scruples, fully changing the nature of what was earlier perceived as fear. In this sense, fears are not paralyzing emotions, but in fact extremely mobilizing. They are the crown of wisdom.

The ability to perceive true relevance in the realm of humility is no more than a foundation, its ankle. This is because humility is the deep internalization of this capacity, transforming itself into not only an aesthetic exercise of this skill but a way of life. In other words, a humble person can live the "fear of God" without having to resort to an air of wisdom or the proud awareness of being wise.

This is why the Jewish tradition recognizes that, although there are many sages in this world, few are true apprentices of humility, and only thirty-six* exist in every generation.

To become wise is to be able erase the fool within us; to become humble is to erase all trace of the wicked one in ourselves. The sage eliminates the dimension of jealousy; the humble one eliminates the dimension of envy and "clothes the Emperor." The following is reserved for the humble, according to Proverbs (22:4): "The effect of humility is fear of the Lord, wealth, honor, and life."

Cosmic Conflict between Mondays and Tuesdays

Another mythical image about hatred, preserved in Jewish tradition, has to do with the violent process of transformation represented in the days of Creation. This image is based on the idea that unity is the fundamental

---

*According to Jewish tradition, each generation is preserved by the existence of thirty-six just people. This idea is derived from a verse of Isaiah (30:18), where the word *lo* ("for Him") is taken for its numerical value, which is 36.

---

source of peace, while dissension and change are responsible for conflict and strife. Here is the reason why we find no variation, discord, or divergence on the first day of Creation, which alludes to divine unity and the creation of homogenous elements such as light. Regarding this day, according to Genesis: "And God saw that it was good."

But on the second day, when important changes are introduced, such as the division of "the waters which were under the firmament from the waters which were above the firmament," there was also the creation of differences, conflict, and dissidence. This is why on the second day there is no mention of the expression of divine pleasure, "it was good." The rabbis say this day marks the moment when differentiation and disputes first arose.

It is interesting to note, however, that on the third day God makes a surprising declaration; twice he expresses his pleasure, as shown by the phrase "and He saw that it was good." In the creation of the earth and the seas and the appearance of vegetation, God consecrates the third day in this very special manner. From here on, to the fourth, fifth, and sixth days, God will repeat his expression of contentment. But on none of these days will it be repeated twice, *"and He saw it was good."* The third day marks the creation of the capacity to live with differences, and the pleasure of it is twofold. After the creation of competitiveness and segregation come cooperation and integration.

After the creation of the shadow representing conflict, as an inherent side effect of difference, came the creation of harmony and the possibility of pacification and integration. This last, perhaps itself the divine reason for having set Creation in motion, produces a level of divine pleasure and satisfaction in superior forms never to be repeated. Even on the day human beings were created, which receives an extra bit of satisfaction from the Creator ("and He saw that it was very good"), cannot wrest from the Heavens two consecutive roars of satisfaction, as were heard on the third day.

As the second day is the only one without the blessing of divine pleasure, it is the source of hatred and discord. The energy of the second day feeds our rancor and envy. This is the source of our blindness to unity in difference, the source of the intolerance, aggression, and destruction that are so much a part of our daily experience.

The third day is the anniversary of the divine surprise that the worlds He was creating were the product of His own essence. Differentiated, separated, and allocated in forms, natures, and creatures, His Creation paid Him homage, by way of an incredible multifaceted reality that was, at the same time, a metaphor of His unity.

On the cosmic level, the energies of unity, dissidence, and harmony are represented in the first days of Creation. As the first day expresses a reality beyond human experience, the second and third days lend themselves as the source of these concrete human feelings. To this day, in Jewish folklore, no kind of initiative or business should be begun on a Monday, or there will be a risk of envy and hatred.* Tuesday is the day that attracts influences of the dimension of patience and tolerance—essential ingredients for those who seek a minimum of quality in life.

Tuesday is also known as *shabbat katan* (the little Sabbath). Saturday, the Sabbath, is symbolic of the utopian world of unity. Its end is marked with a ceremony known as Havdalah, "differentiation." In this ritual, with a return to the normal days of the week, the differentiated nature of this world is emphasized. In order to annul hatred and envy it is essential to know profoundly the condition of difference. We must understand that its nature emanates from the state and form of being of the reality we detect in the Creation itself. Difference is a part of Creation. To be able to honor the different, knowing it to be essentially identical, is like opening one's eyes to the cosmos.

Or, as the rabbis of Yavneh said quite simply:

I am a creature of God and my neighbor is also a creature of God.

I work in the city and he works in the field.

I rise early for my work and he rises early for his.

In the same way that he cannot surpass me in my work, I cannot surpass him in his.

*In the Jewish tradition, a day begins at sunset; thus the second day, Monday, begins at sundown Sunday and ends at sundown Monday.

Would you say that I do great things and he does small things?

We have already learned that it is not important if a person does much or little, as long as his heart is directed to the heavens.

(*Berakhot* 19a)

3

REASONS FOR HATE

We have just seen that rancor grows out of difference or, more precisely, the discovery of difference. Interactions that form deep grudges—as in, "Here, I will lend this to you because I am not like you (who won't lend to me)"—reveal an intense perception of difference and the utilization of it to maintain hatred. In this chapter, we will see some of the most common instances where a perception of difference causes harm. These situations involve a betrayal of the expectation that others are the same.

Children and Disciples, Siblings and Friends

Quite primitively, we despise the people we meet who don't fit into the category of "children and disciples" or "siblings and friends." This phenomenon occurs with different generations (child/disciple) and within the same generation (sibling/friend). Those who we feel are on our team get there for emotional reasons or because of common interests. Expressions such as "So-and-so is like a sister to me" reveal an affective predisposition to esteem; "So-and-so and I are like flesh and blood" reveals esteem arising from a convergence of interests or individual ideologies of disciples or friends.

This primitivism comes from the fact that, as beings with a history of differentiation, we are conditioned to love all we perceive as being part of us or of our essence. All that we love can be boiled down to empathies and interests. As these empathies and interests expand to include more and more of the universe around us, the greater is our sense of internal growth.

Thus love's smallest extension comes down to exclusively loving oneself, a perversion only in relation to an expectation of life within society or collective harmony. All love begins with loving oneself and then seeing in others—children/siblings or disciples/friends—different people who are part of us. Personal growth occurs not out of an attempt to love non-children/siblings or non-disciples/friends, nor from the expectation of betraying our natures, but from a constant review of who we are. This then leads to a search to understand who are our children/siblings and disciples/friends.

The poorer our perception of who we are, the more limited our capacity to include others in one of these two categories. Those who love only themselves, unable to find space for others within themselves, will rarely find children/siblings or disciples/friends in this world.

Rancor is thus partly the product of resistance to growth, or the refusal to include more and more members in our categories of esteem; it also comes from a lack of sensitivity when expressing our differences to others. Rancor arises when we realize that another cannot be a member of our select categories.

Some examples may help to illustrate. The rabbis were very concerned about those who spread secrets:

> A rumor spread that a certain student of Rabbi Ammi revealed a secret confided to him in the house of study twenty-two years before.
>
> For this, Rabbi Ammi expelled him, with the accusation: "This man reveals secrets."
>
> (*Sanhedrin* 31a)

When a person tells someone a secret, it means that he holds his confidant as an equal. But if the confidant reveals the secret, he also reveals himself to be an *outsider*. The energy for the transformation from equal to outsider comes from the second day of Creation. The rabbis say that "a fool with a secret suffers the same agony as a woman in labor." If the one who spread the secret knew that he was about to fortify the forces of the second day and would gradually come to be hated for this, he would think twice before telling.

Another example deals with people who "cop out." The rabbis explain:

> From what verse do we derive the idea that, in leaving a courtroom, a judge should not say, "I believed the accused to be innocent, but my colleagues found him guilty, and what could I do, with them in the majority?"
>
> From the passage in the Scriptures saying: "Do not go spreading stories among your people" (Leviticus 19:16).   (*Sanhedrin* 3:6)

Once again, when we realize that someone is different from others whom we think of as equals, we think of that person as representing difference, and we move away. This example is meant not to stereotype people who tell secrets or those who cop out, but to identify dozens of everyday situations where we send messages about how we distance ourselves from others. In this way, we create fertile spaces for the proliferation of mistrust, dissension, and discord. Obviously, one should not mask these moments, but should instead understand the origin of feelings of estrangement and the perception of difference that others feel about us.

Another kind of situation involves avoiding the revelation of a harsh truth that could serve to foster hate. If we leave out parts of the truth, other people can fill in the resulting empty spaces, absorbing these as painful emotional wounds. The spaces lead others to think of us as radically different from what they thought, to feel betrayed and tricked into regarding us as brothers and sisters or friends. This type of event, common in cases of passion and lovers' betrayals, is caused by people who don't know how to deal with truth to reduce the pain of separation. They often deepen an estrangement by allowing the hurt person to discover the truth on his or her own, creating new spaces of distance and difference, so propitious to rancor and grudges.

Thus so many moments of rancor come from leaving others to the mercy of the second day's energy, leading them to feel difference.

Blushing: Bleeding Inside

The rabbis identified humiliation and the act of shaming a person in public as the most serious reasons for hate, revenge, and the formation of grudges. Making a person blush is an act that can be likened to a stabbing from within. In the Talmud we find the following statement:

> A person who shames [literally "whitens the face of"] another publicly acts as if he has shed blood. To which Reb Naḥman added: "You have spoken well, for we see that the redness of his face disappears and he turns white."   (*Bava Metzia* 58b)

In Reb Naḥman's mind, a shamed person turned pale because he had "lost blood." Whether we are talking about victims of emotional anemia or about bleeding from within, shaming someone in public is not a crime punishable by civil law, though it can be as lethal and destructive as a physical attack. The pain of shame can be worse because shame transcends mere violence to include the lack of compassion. There is a calculated and premeditated element in the act of public humiliation. It is as if the shamed person can anticipate the violence coming his way and, in a fraction of a second, argue with his torturer, begging for mercy. The rabbis provide an excellent example in the following story:

Because of Kamtza and Bar-Kamtza, Jerusalem was destroyed. A man had a friend called Kamtza and an enemy called Bar-Kamtza. Once, he decided to give a banquet and ordered his slave to bring his friend Kamtza. The slave made an error and brought the enemy, Bar-Kamtza. When the owner of the house realized that the man he hated was seated at his banquet table, he said, "You who invent stories about me—what are you doing at my table?" and ordered him to withdraw.

But Bar-Kamtza told him, "Since I am already here, please allow me to stay, and I will pay for whatever I eat and drink."

"No," said the host. Bar-Kamtza begged him, promising, "I will pay for half the banquet if you allow me to stay" [to avoid an embarrassing situation]. The host refused and, taking him by the arm, sent him from his home.

Bar-Kamtza thought to himself, "So many people saw what happened and none protested, which means that they agree with the manner in

which I was treated. For this, I will go to the au-
thorities and turn them in." So he went to the
Roman commander and said, "The Jews have re-
volted against you."   (*Gittin* 55b–56a)

By this account, the destruction of Jerusalem
began with an intrigue involving the public humiliation
suffered by Bar-Kamtza. This story actually relates the
step-by-step transformation of hatred, revealed in the
host's remark, "You who invent stories about me . . . ,"
made in a spirit of revenge. The revengeful remark in
turn ends in the formation of a grudge, in the deep and
symbolic hatred of Bar-Kamtza, rooted in his public humiliation. Such an experience is capable of nothing less
than the destruction of an entire city. In our times, it is
not hard to imagine extending this idea to the whole
planet, threatened as we are by unresolved hatred.

The dramatic peak of our story is Bar-Kamtza's
supplication as he desperately tries to gain his opponent's compassion and mercy. When this doesn't occur,
with the host calculatingly kicking him out, knowing
the pain this will cause, Bar-Kamtza is taken over by
the maximum dimension of hatred. Dominated by the
world of grudges, Bar-Kamtza envies. His envy is sym-
bolically directed against the host and all who witnessed his humiliation. In some form, this envy is
extended to the whole world.

Bar-Kamtza believed that the injustice he had suffered gave him the right and the immunity to hate. Bar-
Kamtza thought the host should bear responsibility for

the consequences, since he had initiated the violence. This would be true if Bar-Kamtza had not voluntarily heightened the conflict, in fact taking on him*self* the responsibility for events to come. Bar-Kamtza's hatred reaches levels far beyond the dimension of hatred felt by the host. This is clearly because Bar-Kamtza's rancor had the power to spill beyond immediate events and even make history; after all, our story begins with the statement "Because of Kamtza and Bar-Kamtza, Jerusalem was destroyed." The host, whose name is unknown, would be the villain of the story if not for Bar-Kamtza's last act.

To summarize, the host is a fool blinded by the world of revenge. Bar-Kamtza, although a victim, becomes wicked. The host is responsible for his foolishness, but this does not justify Bar-Kamtza's attitude. And this is difficult to understand when one is at the center of a conflict.

This story is like that of the child who frantically tries to explain to a parent or teacher that he had nothing to do with a transgression caused by a chain of events he did not set off. It is indeed complicated to understand that we are in fact responsible for the link in the chain that we add and that we may be judged regardless of any immunity we believe we have acquired owing to an injustice that previously victimized us.

Justice is not simply the product of a logic detached from reality. In fact, it is the result of the interaction of many individuals and many realities. Thus we should follow the basic rule of taking great care with attitudes based on rights we believe we possess because of an injustice.

Unfortunately, people involved in conflicts can rarely see this. So often, we catch ourselves or others taking a position that seeks legitimacy in past actions. "He did that, so of *course* I could only react like this. . . ." This is a rationale we ought to be careful with. What the wounded or wronged heart tells us is not always so clear.

We need to understand that we cannot blame others for the greater sense of hatred we feel, while at the same time others must blame themselves for deepening the hatred. Bar-Kamtza's blame comes from having linked a personal dispute to the destruction of Jerusalem. The host carries the blame of having allowed the link of hatred between the two to become a symbolic hatred for everyone. At no time is Bar-Kamtza's attitude legitimated or justified by the host's attitude; but the host should know that at the dramatic moment when his unwelcome guest offers to pay for half the banquet so as to stay, so much tension has been created that he holds the fate of the city in his hands.

Bar-Kamtza could have acted magnanimously and left things as they were, but the host could not count on this. He is responsible, as is anyone who humiliates a person in public, for participating in a chain of hatred, with consequences far beyond what anyone wished for.

One of our duties in the fight against the pollution of rancor in all worlds is to be aware of the destructive power of humiliation, so as to avoid it. But this requires wisdom. The Talmud reveals some examples of sages who knew the art of disarming potential humiliations. One of these is said to be Reb Ḥiyya:

> Once, during a lesson being given by Reb Ye-huda, a strong odor of garlic spread throughout the room. "Whoever ate garlic must leave," said the master. Reb Ḥiyya rose and all the other students followed him out.
>
> The next day, Reb Shimon, son of Reb Ye-huda, asked Reb Ḥiyya, "Did you cause that per-turbing odor?"
>
> "By the Heavens, of course not!" he answered. *(Sanhedrin* 11a)

Another story is told about the Rabbi of Kovno. In a nearby city, a rabbi erred in a judgment over a religious question. He was not aware of the error, but two spiteful individuals were, recalling that an identical case was cited in the rabbinical codes, with a judgment contrary to the rabbi's.

Clearly intending to humiliate the local rabbi, these men wrote a letter to the Rabbi of Kovno, seeking his opinion on a case similar to that judged by the local rabbi. They did this with the certainty that the answer would be different from the local rabbi's, and they planned to show the response around town, to undermine the rabbi's reputation.

When the Rabbi of Kovno received the letter, he

was surprised. After all, he had never before been consulted by these men. Besides, why were they raising a question that any rabbi, including their own local one, could answer?

The Rabbi of Kovno, beginning to suspect a hidden agenda behind the request, asked a few questions. When he discovered what had happened, he decided to answer the letter with the same incorrect answer given by the local rabbi. But the next day, he sent a telegram, meant to arrive before the letter, saying that the solution given in the letter was erroneous, the true one being that given in the rabbinical code. In this manner, the two evil-minded individuals were left without an argument. If the Rabbi of Kovno could err, so could the local rabbi.

These are examples which the true sages keep in mind, making a constant effort to wipe out hatred disseminated in the form of public humiliation. If we become a bit more sensitive to these issues, we will feel a tangible improvement in the quality of our lives and the lives of those around us.

Gossip: The Hate Grapevine

Gossip, the mean-spirited transmission of information, is one of the most important networks for the preservation and transport of rancor. Malicious word-of-mouth is so much a part of daily routine that once again we may find it helpful to make use of the four-world model, to better understand it (see the chart on page 34).

Jewish tradition classifies gossip in three categories: the "evil tongue" (*lashon ha-ra*), tale-bearing (*rekhil* or *rekhilut*), and slander (*motzi shem ra*).

Slander exemplifies the simple case of someone who propagates a lie about another person. The tale-bearer transmits true information with an intent to belittle or malign someone. And the evil tongue—sometimes referred to in the Talmud as the "dust of the evil-tongued"—passes on information told by a third party, while falsely claiming innocence of any hidden motives in doing so.

Maimonides, the twelfth-century philosopher, helps us to understand the difference between the tale-bearer, the evil-tongued, and the dust of the evil-tongued.

> Who is a tale-bearer? The one who spreads gossip, going from one person to another, saying: "This is what So-and-so said about you." "This is what I heard from So-and-so." Even if it is true, it brings about the destruction of the world.
>
> The evil tongue is committed by one who speaks disparagingly of another. Though it is true, . . . when in the company of others, he will say, "So-and-so did this, this is what his parents are, and this is what I've heard about him," uttering disparaging remarks.
>
> The dust of the evil-tongued one says: "Who would have guessed that So-and-so would get to where he is today?" or "Don't talk about So-and-so, I don't even want to remember what

happened"—and then goes on to tell the story. It
is a grave fault to pretend not to realize when one
is being malicious.

This example illustrates that, by ranking the different ways of manipulating information as they relate
to the different worlds of the Kabbalah, we find just the
opposite of what we might expect. Jewish tradition takes
into account the subtlety of these different forms of intrigue, identifying the evil tongue as the most harmful
of all, followed by the tale-bearing, with slander coming
last.

Both the slanderer and the tale-bearer share a
wish to malign people whom they judge as deserving
such treatment. Both feed on the justification that they
cannot pass up an opportunity to denounce those who
have acted erroneously. Thus, in terms of maintaining
hatred, they are very similar instruments.

At first glance, it would appear that the difference
in the type of misdemeanors they commit—one lying
and the other revealing the truth—would define slander
as the worse of the two. But this is not the case. Of
course, the slanderer is responsible for the damage and
consequences of his acts, but the destructiveness of his
malice is less than that of the tale-bearer.

The slanderer falls into the category of *nothing*.
His lie is the solution to the rehabilitation of his victim.
As his lie is revealed, his victim's reputation is immediately restored. This is why the slanderer's intent is in-
finitely less subtle than that of the tale-bearer.

The tale-bearer uses truth as an instrument to deepen intrigue, with a sophisticated sort of malice. Once what is being said is verified, the underlying intent is more likely to feed the spread of rancor. Compared to the tale-bearer, the evil-tongued takes on the role of the *fool*. His desire to malign can also be neutralized by anyone who has the slightest bit of judgment and can question what interests led someone to relate such facts to others.

The evil tongue (and its dust) is our greatest villain. This behavior falls into the dimension of the wicked. Pretending impartiality, the evil-tongued masks his interests. He passes along facts, leaving his listeners to judge for themselves. But the choices of a certain moment and a certain manner in which to pass on information contain elements which are easy fodder for hatreds and grudges.

As the evil-tongued person appears not to possess a hidden agenda, this subliminal element leads the hearer of the gossip to unknowingly assimilate information infected with rancor. Once he has decoded it, he mistakenly believes himself to be the author of a judgment that was in fact already built into the information. The evil-tongued plays the most harmful and endemic role in the transportation and preservation of rancor, since most people practice this habit unaware of its destructive power.

Rabbinical tradition also recognizes that gossip depends on those who lend their ears to it. We are alerted to take care not only to avoid the thoughtless spreading of "stories," but also to learn not to listen to them.

> Know that one who hears a malicious statement is as wicked as one who transmits it. The simple act of paying attention leads those who are nearby to think: "So-and-so listened to what they said and agreed, so what they said must be true."
>
> Even if the listener merely turns his face in the direction of the gossiper and gives the impression of paying attention, this helps to spread intrigue and encourage the latter to continue with such malice.   (*Shaarei Teshuvah*)

This fact is key to identifying the structure of gossip, which spreads via a network built on the availability of listeners, to unleash processes preserving rancor and hatred. Everyone, some more and some less, takes part in this informal network, whose costs to world peace are incalculable.

Breaking with this organized network requires wisdom and discipline. Above all, we must realize that its main efficacy resides in the subtle and tricky ways it distorts our personal values and behaviors, constantly deceiving us. Otherwise, we become the hosts and receptacles of rancor. The stratagems of intrigue are not in the essence of what is said, but in the form in which it is transmitted. For this reason, we are warned that even flattery and praise may contain as much venom as blasphemy.

It is told that once Reb Shimon brought a divorce document to his father, Reb Yehuda, who suspected its validity. "There is no date on this document."

Reb Shimon explained, "Maybe it's on the back." Reb Yehuda looked and found the date. Then he looked at his son in reproof. Reb Shimon hastened to add, ' "It was not I who wrote that, but Yonah, the tailor.' About this, Reb Yehuda replied, "You can leave out the slander."

On another occasion, Reb Shimon was seated next to his father, reading a scroll containing the Book of Psalms. Reb Yehuda commented, "What beautiful handwriting." To which Reb Shimon responded, "It was not I who wrote that, but Yonah, the tailor." His father once again warned him, "You can leave out the slander."

The reason Reb Yehuda scolded his son on the first occasion is obvious. But in the episode where Reb Shimon said that the praised handwriting was the tailor's, why was he told to omit the slander? The reason is that Reb Dimi had taught that we should not engage in the adulation and flattery of others, as it is probable that we will also be tempted to speak of their faults and weaknesses.   (*Bava Batra* 164b)

Adulation is an invitation to envy. Both those who express the praise and those who hear it feel seduced by the desire to diminish the subject of the flattery. Many times, praise opens the path to malice. And what determines the level of intrigue is how we use the information, more than its content. Whether the information is true or false, whether it exalts or disparages, its potential for the transmission of rancor lies in the way it is handled and in the motives it hides. We should not allow ourselves to be bewitched by the superficial appearance of praise.

One question remains: how can we then criticize or censure a person? How can we be sure that we are not really doing it to create intrigue?

Rabbi Israel Meir (1838–1933), known as the Ḥafetz Ḥayyim ("Eager for Life"), dedicated himself to writing about the issue of speech and the criteria for revealing its stratagems. His nickname comes from the verse in Psalm 34 that states, "Who is the man who is eager for life? . . . Keep your tongue from evil and your lips from deceit."

Reb Israel Meir tried to sketch out a brief manual of guidelines for filtering out the pollution of rancor and malice contained in the wish to criticize a person. Here is his formula for being certain our intentions are constructive:

1. Evidence of dishonesty or faults must be obtained by the person who makes the criticism and not by way of rumors he has heard.

2. The person who criticizes must be cautious and reflect deeply on the matter, to be sure that this is an instance of an incorrect attitude.

3. He must then privately censure the person who committed the error, without creating a

furor and in a nonthreatening manner, showing his expectation that the behavior in question will be changed. If this does not occur, then he may make the case public.

4. He should never make the offense appear greater than it is.

5. He should try to understand his own motives and be sure he is not criticizing the other for personal reasons, but is doing this in good faith and with the objective of being constructive.

6. If there is any other way to avoid slandering the other, he should first resort to that method.

7. As a result of his action, he should not bring upon the criticized individual a punishment greater than that proffered by a court if the case were to be judged.

In addition to all this, a person who publicly slanders someone should himself be honest and not guilty of the same type of crimes or faults for which he is criticizing the other. . . . He should also be sure that the people to whom he denounces the fault are not themselves guilty of indulging in practices similar to that being criticized.

Stepping on Toes

A disciple once sought out his teacher to complain that he was always the object of petty aggressions and disrespect. Puzzled, he protested, "Reb, why is that wherever I go, someone is always stepping on my toes?" The rabbi replied without hesitation, "It's because you occupy so much space that people have no choice but to step on your toes!"

We should never forget about our animal dimension. Like any other species in this realm, we need space to live. This is our survival territory. In it we feed expectations that get mixed up with our very identity. This is our area of influence. Anyone who intrudes without authorization instantly turns into an enemy.

Realization of this is crucial. We may act in ways that are totally acceptable under normal conditions. But in foreign territory, our actions take on new meanings. A comment, or the mere monopolization of attention, enacted in the clearly marked territory of another, can generate hatred, jealousy, and envy that are not easily neutralized.

Situations involving groups or third parties are often ripe for this kind of event. Failing to respect the territorial division underlying interaction, we are unaware of the violence we commit. We may realize what is going on only in the wake of an aggressive reaction that initially leaves us perplexed, puzzled about its origin.

A clear-headed person ought to take the same care with other people as he would on entering a new group or culture. In an Indian hut or sitting down for a meal with a Yemenite family, we are sensitive to the need to behave according to the written and unwritten rules of that culture. Even in relation to others belonging to our own culture, we also enter new territory. Without due awareness and respect for the spaces we invade, we commit many *faux pas*.

Once, at a café table, a parent made this comment to a childless couple seated opposite him: "It's so great to be a father." Seeing that they ignored his comment, he repeated it. Soon he was the object of insults. Probably he left the café thinking he was the victim of ill-mannered, unbalanced people. He didn't realize that his apparently harmless comment, in foreign territory, was injurious. Not realizing that this was a sore point for the couple, he was ignorant of the territory of his interaction, and, as usually happens in such cases, he started a feud. If he had had any idea of the cost of his comment, he would not have made it or repeated it.

At moments like this, we should think about what led the other to hate us. Many conflicts where we feel our position is totally justified, when we could swear we did nothing to lead another person to become our adversary, begin with a lack of sensitivity about territory. These territories are in fact fundamental to the way the world works, and no one who seeks wisdom can ignore them. But those who are aware of them can travel through, making the most of what lies within their borders.

People step on others' toes all the time. Even a choice of words can create difficulties in different territories. For example, a mother hearing a suggestion regarding her child is put in a situation where she may feel judged about the love she feels for the child. She may resist the suggestion and feel very little empathy. But if we make the suggestion so as to allow her space within her own maternal territory to deal with the situation, she will certainly manage to listen without rancor. We mustn't forget that motherhood, like many other human conditions, is a territory.

When people step on our toes, many times they do it because we have left no other space for them to stand, except on our own feet.

Taking It Personally

> Words should be weighed, not counted!
> —*Yiddish proverb*

We have seen that implicit forms of violence can often cause greater long-term discord than direct and incontestable violence. The lack of concrete elements in these conflicts blocks the way to clearing up the misunderstanding that initiated a falling-out.

To neutralize the "virus" of this kind of hatred, we must use the mezuzah (keeper of the gates), of both the mind and the heart. Thus we need to be able to deal with doubts about how real the affront is, and know how to recognize when to take something personally. Taking words or actions personally has everything to do with allowing ourselves to enter the world of envy and grudges. Resistance to such a move is a typical reaction of the mezuzah-antibodies of our hearts and minds when they are faced with the possibility of yielding to rancor that could install itself within them.

The kind of rancor wrapped in doubt is extremely disturbing. Although we may act as though we are fully taking an affront personally, inside we are corroded by ambivalence. Doubt about whether hatred for someone is legitimate or not takes us on long journeys of fantasy, when we perceive the length and breadth of the injustice we may be committing. At the same time, these fantasies are filled with voices and images that assure us, through repeating scenes or dialogues, of the authenticity of our feelings. In such a situation, we are bound to have problems.

The following question was posed to Rabbi Alashkar in the fifteenth century:

> A man was arguing with a friend, and in the middle of what the friend was saying, the man shouted, "I am not a hypocrite! I am not shameless! I have character!"
>
> The question was asked: Don't these words imply that his friend is a hypocrite, shameless, and without character? Couldn't we infer this by interpreting his words as follows: "I am not a hypocrite *like you* . . ." and so forth?
>
> The rabbi replied: "It seems to me that the words of this man carry a nonverbal implication of the type 'I am not a such-and-such like you.' After all, his companion did not accuse him of being a hypocrite or shameless. There is no reason for him to deny these allegations, except with

the intent that the listener infer: 'I am not one,
but you are.'

This can be associated with a mention in the Talmud (*Bava Metzia* 33a). This text discusses certain
questions relating to the affirmation that a teacher must
be shown more respect than a father. The Talmud tells
us that Reb Ḥisda asked his own teacher, Reb Huna,
"What kind of respect should be shown by a disciple
whose teacher needs him as much as he needs the
teacher?"

Reb Huna took the question personally and
shouted, "Ḥisda, Ḥisda, I do not need you, but you will
need me until you are forty!" Feelings hurt, they did
not speak to each other for many years after this.

Even though Reb Ḥisda may not have meant his
words as an to insult his teacher, Reb Huna understood
them to carry malicious intent, and from his point of
view they were as destructive as if he had been openly
insulted.

The situation is similar in the case described earlier. It is as if the man had openly declared, "I am not
such-and-such, as you are." He insulted his friend
without verbalizing an insult (Moshe ben Yitzhak
Alashkar, *Response*, n. 81).

In fact, we often offend others nonverbally, many
times even less explicitly than in the Talmud story. Attitudes, gestures, looks, associations, or any other action
that speaks for us can be an instrument of insult.

Responsibility begins in the hands of the person

who makes the potential personal attack. Even if he or she is absolutely certain of not intending an offense, offense was given. The weight of a nonoffense that offends is the same as a true offense. But once again, the dimension of grudges is only evoked by the person who finds himself offended or has doubts about whether or not he was offended. This is the person who carries the fantasies, who goes over and over situations in his mind, and who, if he does not act openly to wreak vengeance, will certainly send dubious messages evidencing his rancor.

From the point of view of the person who took things personally, what matters is proof that he truly was the target of violence or offense. All his rancor is centered on the certainty that he was the object of attack. Thus in every such situation it is important to realize the dangerous dimension of rancor we evoke when taking things personally, and then to identify the true object of aggression. If we can develop the ability to perceive that in many cases the attack comes from people who are under stress or oppressed by their world, or suffering from internal fears or insecurities, we discover that we are the misplaced victim of feelings meant for a wife, father, sister, or some other. Those who can see farther come to understand that an act of aggression may not have been as personal as they may have thought.

Psychology and other behavioral studies teach a great deal about the projection of feelings that have become detached from their true sources. If I am attacked by someone who argued with his boss, perhaps I can understand that his attitude, though violent, was not meant personally.

What difference does this make? A great deal. The identification of an offense that was not meant personally closes the door to the dimension of grudges. Of course, the attack itself is a reality. But we are in the sphere of simple hate or, in the worst hypothesis, the sphere of revenge. Here, the chances of starting a feud are smaller, because this depends on a belief that an offense was meant personally. Both envy and grudges grow like parasites on feelings of personal hatred.

We are dealing here with the sphere of the *ear* and the *mouth*. In the area of the mouth, the aggressor has established the level of netirah (grudges): "I am not like you." It is in the dimension of the ear, however, that the existence or absence of the notion of "personal" will determine whether the conflict will become a feud or a less lasting form of hatred.

The last word on a conflict lies in the ear. Clear speech is important for avoiding misunderstandings, but clear listening is even more important. Even those who speak in an unclear manner may still find an ear that hears accurately.

Here is the reason for the Shema, the central prayer of Jewish tradition: "Hear O Israel, the Lord is our God, the Lord is One." Listen and don't speak. The act of speaking does not make a witness, but listening does. The ear can speak more than mouths do.

Thus the same can be said about someone who

hears something with a personal cast. Taking criticism personally is a very serious decision. If the ear was wrong, this will be a worse error than that which came from the mouth of the person who made the comment.

Only when it falls silent can the mouth equal the destructiveness of the ear. Later we will see how a silent mouth that keeps rancor to itself is seen through the prism of envy and hatred, like an ear.

In Jewish tradition, a person who speaks is like an archer: He shoots his arrows, and once they are in the air, he cannot wish them back into the bow. He has created, he realizes later, emissaries or extensions of himself with the powerful capacity to act in his name. All attitudes and consequences caused by these agents will be his responsibility. He who perceives this knows the art of saying little.

But someone who takes things personally walks through the forest and, wherever he sees an arrow stuck in a tree, draws a target around it.* His perception of reality leads him to believe the aggression was obviously intentional and premeditated. His target with an arrow stuck right in the middle is lasting proof of his illusion.

---

*An allusion to a parable of the Dubner Maggid, about an archer who appears amazingly to have shot a series of bull's-eyes but who actually shot the arrows first and then drew the targets around them.

4

QUARRELING

If the heart is bitter, nothing will sweeten the mouth.
—Yiddish proverb

Triple Tears

Great feuds are not the product of mere greed or of simple disputes over acquisitions. They involve, as we have seen, the symbolic plane of envy. Here we see that the enemy or the source of disagreement exists not in the real world, but in that of interaction. In all hatred, a personal component distorts our perceptions, intensifying the weaknesses of the other, even when these are real. Another observer may perceive those very weaknesses as a cause for admiration, not rejection. A repressed person seeking to change himself may admire the sensual behavior of another individual, while this same characteristic brings hatred from a third individual who is at that same moment looking to repress his behavior.

Thus we may deeply hate something in others that we do not like in ourselves, or something in others that reminds us of our frustrations, and so forth. In the immediate interests of thinking about *quarreling*, we want to identify this element residing in those who hate, signaling a strong link with the object of that emotion. No one takes his hatred as far as a feud unless he is strongly linked to the person he hates. Understanding this is fundamental to the analysis of a disagreement. The Maggid of Mezeritz said:

> Do not be discouraged by strong opposition. Robbers attack those who carry jewels, not carts carrying fertilizer. We must think of ourselves as carriers of jewels, in order to repel robbers.

People whom we hate carry "jewels" in the sense of something that interests us, something important to us. These jewels can be good or evil, but to the robber they symbolize an object of great desire. Both the robber and the victim must be aware of this. The Maggid of Mezeritz even risks the suggestion that, in reacting to violence, the individual under attack should not forget to think of himself as a carrier of jewels. When we are not aware of this, we may erroneously take personally much of what is sent in our direction. We are merely carriers of jewels, in the eyes of the other—jewels we may not even perceive.

The greater the importance of the carrier or of his jewels, the greater the violence with which he may be assaulted. There are many examples. Of all biblical feuds, the most intense, the one clearly demonstrating elements of the structure of hatred, is the feud between Jacob and his brother Esau. Jacob, helped by his mother, Rebecca, craftily and calculatedly manages to steal the birthright and the blessing that by rights belong to Esau. There is no worse or more tempestuous cause of envy and feuding. Here is the perfect environment for the growth of great hatred and grudges. This is so true that before Esau swears to kill his brother, pouring out his hatred, he is invaded by an emotion foreshadowing the start of the feud, the "triple tears."

The Bible describes Esau's reaction to the betrayal: ". . . he cried out with a great and bitter cry" (Genesis 27:34). Esau's cry came to symbolize the extreme pain of hatred regarding someone important to us, a person who "carries jewels."

The eleventh-century commentator Rashi, on reading the verse of Psalms (80:6), "You feed them with the bread of tears and give them tears to drink in three measures," associated these tears with those poured forth by Esau. Rashi remembered the above verse, describing the reaction of immediate pain felt by Esau. "He cried out" is the first dimension of the tear; "great" is the second; and "bitter" is the third. This three-dimensional tear symbolizes the greatest pain of hatred. Its first dimension (cry out) is about the pain of privation of something desired; the second (great) refers to the deepening of pain owing to the specific personality of Jacob, which underscored weaknesses intrinsic to Esau himself; and the third (bitter) had to do with Jacob being his brother, the factors of proximity and competitiveness also increasing his pain.

With the triple tears, we can map the entire structure of hatred from the viewpoint of the one who is offended or wounded. A double tear, made up of "cry out" and "great," a misunderstanding that is immediately taken personally, is in itself enough to start a feud. The triple tears are even more powerful and start extremely complex, emotionally sophisticated feuds that are hard to end. Usually these occur among families or former friends. Thus, the greater the knowledge and proximity between two people, the more careful they must be if a conflict arises, as they are candidates for causing or suffering "triple tears."

The Talmud (*Bava Metzia* 84a) tells about two dear friends, Rabbi Yohanan and Resh Lakish. The latter was a professional gladiator who changed his whole life because of the friendship, becoming a student of Rabbi Yohanan. Here is the story of the feud between them:

> One day Rabbi Yohanan was bathing in the River Jordan when Resh Lakish passed by. Rabbi Yohanan said, "Such strength—if only it could be devoted to study of the Torah!"
>
> "Your good looks," replied Resh Lakish, "should be for women."

Then Rabbi Yoḥanan said, "If you repent and change your life, I will allow you to marry my sister, who is even more good-looking than I." So Resh Lakish changed his life, married the sister, and went to study with his brother-in-law, who taught him about holy books.

One day, there was a dispute in the house of study about certain tools—the sword, the knife, the dagger, and the sickle—and whether they were considered ritually pure. Rabbi Yoḥanan claimed they were, as long as they had been passed through the fire of an oven. Resh Lakish claimed they were as long as they had been washed with water.

Rabbi Yoḥanan spoke hastily: "A thief knows his trade" (referring to Resh Lakish's use of these tools in his previous occupation as a gladiator).

To which Resh Lakish responded with hatred: "And how much did you really help me? There [in the Roman circus] I was known as master, and here I am too."

Rabbi Yoḥanan felt deeply wounded by the implication that he had not helped Resh Lakish and refused to forgive him. Thus Resh Lakish fell ill and died soon after.

Rabbi Yoḥanan feel into a deep depression, tearing his clothing and weeping copiously, crying, "Where are you, son of Lakisha? Where are you, son of Lakisha?" until he went mad. The rabbis prayed that he might be freed from his misery, and soon after he also died.

The most impressive aspect of this story is how people who complement each other, or people who admire each other and need each other very much, can quarrel so easily. Between friends who give much to each other, a sense of betrayal and ingratitude is unbearable. If we trace with Rabbi Yohanan the path of his hatred, as he sits facing Resh Lakish, we hear the student express himself with confidence, repeating phrases and ideas that Rabbi Yohanan taught him. For reasons of his own, Rabbi Yohanan felt threatened by Resh Lakish's power. Watching him as he spoke, he felt hatred. It was a normal hatred, that of a person who says to himself, "Who taught him all this, if not I? He speaks as if these were his own words; does n't he realize he owes it all to me?"

If Resh Lakish had realized this, he would have been able, with just a word of gratitude to Rabbi Yohanan, to prevent his teacher's ire. More than this, he would have been able to transform it into pure affection and love. This is because hatred, in the instant before it hardens, is a material easily molded into love, as long as the correct chemistry is utilized. For a few moments, Rabbi Yohanan held back his malicious comment. But the more he resisted, the greater was the temptation.

When Rabbi Yohanan pronounces his finding about the tools being ritually pure or impure, and hears Resh Lakish contest it, the blood rises to his head. He feels stabbed inside, bleeding within. He blurts out a comment on Resh Lakish's past, which, to the initiated listener, is a clear sign of jealousy. Rabbi Yohanan was already emotionally needy before he felt attacked by his friend's dissent. At that instant, he could not resist, and began a process that greatly endangers a friendship.

On the other hand, if we trace the path of Resh Lakish's hatred, we find that he flirted with his knowledge in a love triangle of which Rabbi Yohanan was still the main apex. In front of his teacher-friend, he showed off what he had learned. Rabbi Yohanan unfortunately did not realize that his pupil's attitude was a form of homage to the teacher who had offered him the chance to change his life. Resh Lakish most likely wanted to show that he was as able as his teacher, and thought to renegotiate his friendship. He wanted to review the relationship of gratitude, to update it in another form. Rabbi Yohanan refused, however. Instead of recognizing Resh Lakish as a teacher as well, Rabbi Yohanan preferred to remind him of the fact that he had been a gladiator not long before. The only way Resh Lakish found to return the blow was to reinforce his position, whereby friendship based on gratitude tends to weaken.

"No, I am not grateful! After all, why would I be? If they call me master here, there they also do!" The violence which Rabbi Yohanan perceives in these words is clear evidence that both friends are no longer in the dimension of jealousy, but that of envy.

Neither man was able to recognize that they were fighting over their friendship; they disagreed about how to continue with it, and they shed triple tears. For a few fatal moments, they fooled themselves into thinking they were enemies. They paid dearly for their inability to negotiate their love and its needs.

Quarreling with God

A side effect of the two rabbis' feud was severe depression. The fact that Rabbi Yohanan distanced himself from Resh Lakish indicates that they spent long years hating each other. This is a form of hatred that reveals much about the expectations of those who quarrel. The act of entering a conflict carries with it a deep conviction regarding ultimate victory. No one enters into a feud thinking he will lose the fight. This "theology of victory"—the belief that one side will manage to prove to the other that he or she is right and that the other will end up begging forgiveness—is what maintains a feud. But the certainty of victory is a setup for repeated disillusionment. Depression revives the pain of the triple tears and drowns the individual in blame, longing, and nostalgia.

The history of the feud and the quarrel is similar to the rabbis' description of the "evil inclination" (*yetzer ha-ra*): "The evil inclination works in two ways: like water that cools the desire to do good deeds, and like fire that heats the desire to do wrong."

Likewise, the wish to come to an understanding and resolve the issues at stake is constantly cooled, while the compulsion toward aggression is heated. Time passes, depression takes over, and tragic endings like that in our story become possible.

The costs of such quarrels are incalculable, because they harm the planet's well-being to a frightening degree. The destruction is so overwhelming that even when the effects are not as concrete as they were for the two friends, it disrupts and embitters entire lives.

This is what happened to Jacob and his brother Esau. Because of their feud, the brothers were parted for twenty-one years of resentment, and Jacob found himself distanced from the parents he loved so much, especially his mother. In exile, he began his adult life alone and started a family far away from his native land.

To overcome the curse of his feud, Jacob underwent one of the most intense experiences of the entire Bible, struggling with God. The biblical text tells of his meeting with his brother, when he still feared revenge. Jacob spent the night before this alone, on the far side of the Jaboc (Jabbok) River. There, in the dark of the night, he was visited by a puzzling figure with whom he wrestled. First appearing as a man, Jacob's contender slowly revealed himself as an angel, or even God Himself. This was a symbolic fight, as is every fight to win a feud. Jacob would think he was fighting his brother and discover he was fighting with God. At dawn, after the night of catharsis, Jacob received a new name, symbolic of the great transformation he had undergone. The new day brought a new Jacob. His name came to be Israel: he who fights (*yisra*) with God (*El*). Jacob had to come to a river whose name is an anagram formed by the inversion of the letters in his own name (*J-c-b; J-b-c*), to be able to understand himself, undertaking a return to a reverse of himself. The Jaboc River had given him the insight that his adversary was no longer his brother, but God.

God represents what we believe, the structure of being and thinking we are tied to. This constantly dies and revives as a new paradigm of our faith and belief. We repeatedly find that our prior God was not God, but an allusion to the Divine, and this is something we understand and perceive more after our quarrels.

Jacob discovered that the conflict he had kept up with his brother for so many years was in fact a conflict within himself. His name would thereafter be changed, and the karma of the name "Israel" would be linked to the ability to undertake this difficult struggle. It is difficult because it demands that we identify within ourselves the shadows of men and women who are not external individuals, but shadow parts of ourselves. Jacob knows what he is talking about when, meeting up with his brother once again, he exclaims, "Seeing your face is like seeing the face of God" (Genesis 33:10).

Being able to fight with our God, with our deepest internal structure and our eye on the world at large, is the only way to end a feud. In Rabbi Yoḥanan and Resh Lakish's situation, understanding this is very difficult. For each one, from each point of view, ending the conflict is impossible. As in all conflicts, the fact that the two men seek different kinds of relationships with each other appears to prevent any sort of reconciliation. The act of fighting with God—that is, totally changing one's assimilated perspective—comes either with wisdom and personal growth, or with time. Time can foster a sense of irony, which does away with the petty ghosts inside us who once felt so real.

Yet it is sad when our internal time is not in tune with fate and we find ourselves in Rabbi Yoḥanan's desperate situation. His friend died before he could fight with God. What remained was a chance for an internal struggle, although he would be forever deprived of the incredible experience of looking at his friend's face and understanding that it was as if he was "seeing the face of God."

"I'm Right"

> Truth neither lives nor dies; it tries to survive!
> —*Yiddish proverb*

When we are imprisoned in the dimension of quarreling, one of the greatest illusions is the sense of being in the right. We create a circular consciousness of the situation, tied only to itself. No matter how much we try, we cannot move beyond the circle. Hoping to confirm our reading of the behavior we find wholly inconceivable, we seek the opinion of third parties. When we become certain by way of our own discernment and the backup of those we have consulted, we face a frightening reality. If the other person's position is unfounded and he still stands by it, we conclude that he must be bad. He must be part of the world that sees things backwards. We think, "It's because of people like him that the world is the way it is!" And we go on with our conjectures. "If I'm right, then there's no solution to the conflict, except for the other guy to renounce his position."

The feeling of being on the side of justice, being in the right, may be a legitimate opinion, but not a certainty. Both total confidence in our judgment and the obsessive search to prove that the other is wrong have two negative consequences: accusation and self-justification. The rabbis explained:

> When you accuse someone and pronounce judgment on this person, saying he deserves this or that, you are pronouncing judgment on yourself. Although the other person's error is foreign to your manner of being and behaving, you will have already committed this same error, in a similar way. If you accuse someone of idol worship, for example, you will certainly be blamed for pride— which is in itself a form of idol worship. And your error may even be bigger than the one you point out, since the judgment on you will be even more severe and critical. But if you justify the person who is wrong, pardoning him because he is still imprisoned in his incarnation and cannot control his desires, then you will be justifying yourself.

The warning is clear. At the moment of judgment, we are always subject to an internal agenda, to interests that justify us, underlying any thought of impartiality. In other words, the feeling of being right on a particular issue involves an attempt to legitimate our own way of being. We always end up setting criteria for our judgments based on who we are and what our interests may be. When judging someone's behavior, rarely do we put ourselves on the line or seek any kind of personal transformation. Even when spurred by an attempt at self-improvement and discernment, such comparisons are difficult; they are even less accessible when our potential weaknesses are exposed to others. Thus we are not to be fully trusted in the midst of a quarrel, and we should always suspect our certainties. They will often veil painful difficulties.

One paralyzing argument remains to strengthen the defensive, intransigent positions of those who quarrel. If we are so untrustworthy in any conflict, an opinion is an impossibility. According to this argument, there is no space for any assertion and all communication should be shut down from the start.

This is a very persuasive point, since it astutely tries to lead those involved in a conflict to think that they have no right to an opinion. Its power to distort lies precisely in the true part of its affirmation: without individuals, there is no dialogue. An old Yiddish saying attests to this:

> So I am I because you are you; and you are you because I am I—so neither I am I, nor you are you. But I am I because I am I; and you are you because you are you—so I am I and you are you, and we can talk to each other!

Dialogue can only exist when "I am I and you are you." The saying reveals the great secret which the above argument tries to cover up. For legitimate conflict to take place, you must be you not because the other is the other. In other words, as we have seen, a person's position in an argument should not entail any criticism he would be reluctant to make of himself, nor any justification of his own behavior. Otherwise, he gets caught up in an identity formed in the shadow of others, involving himself in the armor and arguments of a false ego. He crosses the limit between himself and the other, or the group, touching on the dimension of envy, symbolic hatred. This mistake of getting mixed up with others' identities is the source of the violence of feuds, partiality, and malicious tale-bearing.

To be able to develop a capacity to be oneself "because I am I" is a very secret, esoteric formula, a contribution to the age of the messiah. This era of perfect communication will not be attained by the efforts of a single individual, but by that of many individuals. This is because the other must be other (in terms of his or her own self), in order for dialogue to take place.

For the time being, in this unredeemed world, while we await the coming of the era of the ideal dialogue, we can do much by working towards "I am I because I am I." This is the true dimension of justice in an imperfect world without true dialogue. Being just means not being blind to difference or arguing against dissent, but ensuring that discord is legitimate, without projections or contamination on the part of others.

Being just is being assertive when all interests conspire to a contrary position, avoiding the temptation to shape reality to one's own opinions. The benefit of the doubt (judging people innocent until they are proven guilty) and constant suspicion regarding the interference of personal issues are indispensable protectors for those who may feel they are in the right.

Being right lies on a tenuous line between true worship and idol worship. On the one hand, it is a feeling to avoid, one that allows detours and perversions, strengthening false perceptions of self and blocking dialogue. On the other hand, it is the posture of the sage and the just, since knowing when to make a correct choice, without allowing corruption by interests and personal needs, is one of the most difficult human challenges.

We can thus say that there is a constructive form of conflict, where the assertive belief in being right not only helps dialogue, but also defines the task of the just. For centuries, these fundamental sources of discord have been the object of the rabbis' talmudic debate.

Discord for the Sake of Heaven

> All discord for the sake of Heaven is destined to endure; all that is not for Heaven's sake will vanish. . . .
> —*Pirkei Avot*, 5:21

Discord can begin both in love and in hatred. Discord that starts with love occurs when, despite their differences, the contenders share a common sense of integrity. In such cases, each side deeply respects the motivations and opinions of the other.

To become involved in discord for the sake of Heaven, the adversaries must be equally committed to the aim of being right, to agreeing to one definition of what this means. When a just person makes a statement, he must develop a very special posture regarding his assertion. He must reach the complex stage of knowing he is not right, but being certain he is not wrong. This is the sole legitimate posture for taking a stand, for beginning a true dialogue.

Not knowing whether one is right has to do with the capability to listen and seek the truth. The certainty of not being wrong has to do with having confidence in one's own assumptions. This means being committed to values that are not entangled in personal interests or needs. Because there is no absolute truth, the truth itself depends on the assumptions underlying the search for it. This is why people committed to different sets of assumptions cannot relate to each other, and dialogue is impossible.

Thus the truth closest to what we idealize as absolute and universal is the one we can talk through, debating differences with respect for others' opinions, reworking our positions. Anyone committed to less than this dilutes himself with other identities and opinions, and cannot truly be his own person. Dialogue is impossible with such individuals. At the same time, those who are overly committed to their own assumptions are corrupt, and their truths have no dimension beyond themselves. Such small truths cause discord that is not for the sake of Heaven and are destined to disappear.

The Talmud (*Bava Metzia* 59b) gives us an example of this, in an incident about Rabbi Eliezer and a group of other rabbis:

> Rabbi Eliezer used all his arguments to try to convince a group of rabbis of his view, but they did not accept it. Then he exclaimed, "If that's how it is, let this tree prove that the law is as I say!"
>
> The tree moved instantly from one side to the other, a distance of about fifty meters. His colleagues scorned the feat, saying, "This tree proves nothing!"
>
> Rabbi Eliezer replied, "Let this stream prove that the law prevails according to my opinion!" Soon the current reversed itself. Still the rabbis were not impressed.
>
> Rabbi Eliezer went on: "May the walls of this house show my opinion!" As he finished speaking, the walls of the house began to shake, almost to the point of falling down.
>
> Rabbi Yoshua protested, "If studious people are discussing the law, why are you interfering?" And in respect for Rabbi Yoshua, the walls did not fall down, but, also in deference to Rabbi Eliezer, they did not return to their original position.
>
> Rabbi Eliezer would not give up. "May

Heaven itself announce that the law is as I say!"
And from the Heavens a voice declared, "Why
are you arguing so much with Rabbi Eliezer,
whose opinion should prevail?"

But Rabbi Yoshua cried out, defying the
voice from Heaven, "It is written in the Scriptures
[Deuteronomy 30:12]: 'The law is not in the
Heavens!' "

Rabbi Yermiyah explained that what Rabbi
Yoshua meant was that, since the revelation
[Torah] was given on Mount Sinai, we do not need
any voice from Heaven saying what to do; the
Torah itself gives us the solution [Exodus 23:2]:
Lean to the opinion of the majority!

Sometime later, the Talmud relates, Rabbi
Nathan met the spirit of the prophet Elijah in the
marketplace and asked him how the Eternal reacted when Rabbi Yoshua defied the voice coming from Heaven. Elijah replied, "He smiled
and said, 'My sons denied my motion! My sons
have vanquished me'!"

Absolute truth does not exist as a human criterion
for justice. Only the truth extracted from discord in the
name of Heaven serves this purpose. Rabbi Eliezer
would certainly have his minority opinion respected in
the rabbinical system if he were a participant in discord
for the sake of Heaven, here on earth. Minority opinions
are preserved until today in the Talmud, where different
rabbinical opinions, regardless of whether or not they
were agreed on, are registered. Rabbi Eliezer was not

sure he was not wrong; he just wanted to be right. Not even with the Heavens' consent could absolute right be constructive. Only discord among humans for the sake of Heaven can set standards for justice and Torah.

Striving to be absolutely right is a very common attitude among humans. When we are trying to prove to an adversary that he is totally wrong, we fantasize about a moment when the Heavens, the forces of the cosmos itself, will come to our aid. Like small children, we imagine being able to set fire to the blackboard, to call attention to an injustice on the playground. To our disappointment, the blackboard does not catch fire—or, even if it does, the reaction defies our expectations.

The reality of dissension is that when it is based on and legitimated by human experience, it is not built on right/wrong or hero/villain dichotomies. To be able to overcome it or continue it in the name of Heaven, we must understand that Heaven has no power to resolve discord. This is because the dynamic of such discord is to produce something unknown to and not invented by the Heavens.

We are like children who wish that their parents would come to school one day to teach everyone, for once and for all, who we are. It is painful, but we know this is impossible. Communication can truly take place only within the reality of the school, its playground rules, its etiquette, and its own conventions. A parent's presence in school breaks communication and prevents us from being our true selves.

It is very difficult to deal with the expectation that

justice will be done. Justice does express itself, as the sages say, but in its own time. And even though time seems ungrateful, leaving many situations unresolved, these will persist for as long as they are issues for the sake of Heaven. We will always have the comfort of knowing they won't see closure until they are resolved.

Discord that is not for the sake of Heaven will not last, and the energy spent proving who is right is wasteful, not at all constructive. Knowing when to invest in discord and when to avoid it is a question of economy and intelligence.

5

AVOIDING CONFLICT

There is no deaf man like the one who does not hear,
and there is no blind man like the one who does not
see.

—Yiddish proverb

Knowing How to See

The king visited the royal prison and spoke with
the prisoners. Each who approached vowed his
innocence, except for one prisoner, who con-
fessed to being a thief. "Get this scoundrel out of
here!" exclaimed the king. "He will corrupt the
innocent!"

When we are irate, we can hardly see or breathe.
Our nostrils expand and our eyes contract, as if we
needed more air for our lungs and better focus for our
eyes. This is a very serious moment for an irate individ-

ual, because he is often compelled to act, to take a stand. But good sense tells us that when breathing is difficult, we should rest; when eyesight is poor, we should avoid aiming at targets. It is very important to see the situation clearly!

The greater a reaction of hatred, the more our eyes demand that we focus better on the position we have taken. This is the posture of the wise person—to see clearly. We must first see in terms of ourselves, and then in terms of others in relation to us.

When looking at oneself, the wise person should perceive that hatred is a denser medium than reality, that all feeling passing through it is distorted. Wisdom means knowing, like seagulls, how to correct for detours off a flight path, so as to gain a view undistorted by hatred. The Rabbi of Lublin illustrated this question:

> From youth, Rabbi Teitelbaum was a fervent enemy of the Hasidic doctrine, believing it to be one of the worst forms of heresy. He once visited the home of his friend Rabbi Asher, who also opposed the Hasidic movement and its innovations. At the time, the prayer book of Rabbi Isaac Luria, one of the precursors of the Hasidic doctrine, had just been published.
>
> After some time, a copy of it was brought to the rabbis. Rabbi Teitelbaum quickly grabbed it out of the messenger's hands, tore it up, and threw it on the ground. But Rabbi Asher picked it up from the floor, saying, "After all, it is a prayer book and must not be disrespected."

When the story of this came to the ears of the Rabbi of Lublin, a member of the Hasidic movement, he commented, "Rabbi Teitelbaum will become a member of the Hasidic group; but Rabbi Asher never will. This is because he who burns with hate and enmity today will burn with love for God tomorrow; but the door is closed for the one whose hate is cold and inexpressive."

And what the Lublin Rabbi said came to pass.

Knowing how to recognize an adversary's true characteristics, going beyond immediate attitudes and emotional outbursts, is knowing how to see. The section on taking things personally explained how a deeper reading of an extremely hateful attitude is essential to understanding its roots and reasons.

People frequently react to the surprise of an aggressive act by trying to label it "unreasonable," but in fact hatred always has its reasons. True, we have all experienced moments when irritation has built up and we explode in the face of an "innocent" person. But a deeper reading of such a moment will show that although the innocent person was just a circumstantial receptacle of our wrath, he served as a "ground" for a discharge of anger—and there was a reason for this.

The discharge is a moment of clarity, like a flash of lightning that illuminates human relations. This causes a sudden contraction of the eyes but also releases light through which we can see. That is what the

Lublin Rabbi did. Not letting himself be influenced by the act of aggression, not allowing his eyes to shut in hatred, he left them wide open and witnessed the exposure of a hidden reality.

To the fool, this reality appears as clairvoyance, but it is actually a form of prophecy. Prophecy comes from a wise person's ability to keep his eyes open when everyone else's are closed. He thus sees a world that is not perceived by most people. In the time lost as emotional and spiritual eyes blink, a great wealth of life potential dissipates. This is why feuding—which represents a loss of life—is so sad.

When a wise person sees what the lightning reveals, he must understand that there are criteria of responsibility in aggressive and rancorous interactions. These criteria are defined by a rabbinical concept known as *tinok she-nishbah*, a captive child that does not know of his origin. This concept calls attention to the care we must give to a defenseless child who doesn't even know how to walk by himself—or to a person who cannot see as well as we do.

We must always develop our roles so as to define who is a "minor." A person who can see becomes instantly responsible for the outcome of a controversy. This is how, in the emotional and spiritual world, jurisprudence is established.

Here is the basis for the saying "It takes two to tango." If one party sees himself as an adult and the other as a baby who crawls, there will be no feud.

This is a very useful concept in the deflection of

hatred. If in the heat of a misunderstanding we can build a bridge to a deeper reality, defining each party's capacity to see, we will not allow ourselves to be dragged into the artifices of ire.

It is also important, when identifying oneself as an adult and another as a minor, not to take on superior airs. This is exactly the tenuous line between the ability to appease and the act of diving more deeply into a feud. Being an adult does not award a person greater credit; it merely makes a distinction. For this reason, it is very difficult to be an adult when dealing with a *tinok she-nishbah*. We must do our very best to understand him as product of circumstances, instead of as someone who is not so mature or wise as we are. To really be able to feel this is to *see*.

Thus we perceive that pride is the greatest trap when it comes to the question of vision. We are frequently victims of this situation when we think with ironic indifference of others as objects to be vanquished or reduced. We adopt a false maturity that actually deepens differences.

When one person falsely says he won't fight, two will fight, and a great deal at that!

The Danger of Seeing: A Digression on Human Nature

Knowing how to see is truly a task for sages. Seeing human reactions and attitudes as revealed in a lightning flash is not enough; one must also pay attention to the ghosts of this luminosity. If you don't close your eyes during a flash, and thus perceive deep intentions and motivations, certain images that remain on the retina are not real and must be erased from the portrait of reality engraved on your memory.

Being able to read someone's mind and heart is a very serious matter, because this implies being able to correctly analyze the data furnished by the reading. The danger for those who would be wise lies in the traps set up by his very "wisdom." The fool, as we saw above, is the apprentice of wisdom, legitimating his perception as wise before it attains ripeness. The fool traces a sincere, sensitive path and claims he has reached wisdom when this still lies beyond his grasp, demanding greater perseverance and experience. The fool believes that the lightning flash reveals attitudes and intentions. Attitudes are revealing, but intentions are more so, the fool hastily concludes.

This conclusion is not wrong so much as hasty. There are in fact three levels of revelation: attitudes, intentions, and the intentions of the intentions. To understand this better, a small digression on human nature is necessary.

To claim that we are naturally good, culturally good, seems to be a truism. And while this may be logically true, it may not be true from the point of view of daily perception. For example, a child who appears angel-like may, given access to power, have the potential to become a great tyrant or despot. His ability to relate to others is so undeveloped that he can become merciless with those who fail to satisfy his wishes.

We often forget our animal dimension, and the fact that the development of our divine potential is what permits us to behave with integrity, ethics, and decency. Such reactions are not spontaneous; they come with education, which here includes all the love and compassion given to a person, and all the limits imposed on him so that he conforms to the world and its interactions. Thus there are two kinds of spontaneity: animal and, deriving from education, divine.

Animal spontaneity is what the rabbis called *yetzer ha-ra*, the evil inclination. This is not an absolute, because its negativity exists in opposition to the divine impulse derived from education. Without animal spontaneity, we would neither survive nor procreate. But as they touch upon human relations and exchanges, these impulses can be extremely harmful. Animal spontaneity is so strong that it arises at birth and persists throughout life, until the last breath.

The account handed down to us of a disciple of the great sage and master Isaac Luria (known as the Ari) tells much about the uninterrupted presence of animal spontaneity until death:

> One of the Ari's closest disciples was about to die. His friends and relatives were at his side in the last moments. One of the students present approached the ear of this man in his death throes and asked him, "Does the *yetzer ha-ra* remain with you even now, at this last moment?"

The moribund old man, debilitated and weakened, made a great effort to nod his head: "Yes!"

Surprised, the student inquired, "But what could it be telling you now, at the final moment?"

"The *yetzer ha-ra*," replied the disciple impatiently, "is telling me to recite the Shema [the prayer recited on one's deathbed] aloud, so I can be sure that people will remember me with reverence and will say, 'He died with sanctity and purity on his lips.'"

On his deathbed, a person is still in the company of animal spontaneity, in this case greed or avarice. The rabbi who raises the question is shocked because at that instant, when all is already lost, the dying man still harbors the will to conquer, an interest behind his acts. But he should not be surprised, because we humans do have an animal nature and are always under its influence.

Education creates an intention that may or may not be put into practice. This intention is also spontaneous, although this is not obvious. In other words, the dying man in our story could say the Shema in silence, lest others perceive his desire to show off his devotion; or he could remain silent, having realized that his animal intention was leading him to dishonesty.

In the first option, his attitude would have been to recite in silence, while his (animal) intention would have been to recite aloud, though he chose not to; and the intention of his intention would also be to recite aloud. In the second option, his attitude is also one of silence, but his intention is to recite silently, while the intention of his intention is to recite aloud.

Thus the fool, who knows only the attitude and its intention, confuses intention with the "intention of the intention" (animal intention), believing both to be identical.

Thinking about fantasy may help to clarify this issue. When we fantasize something, we come face to face with a situation that we neither put into practice nor even intend to live out. If we catch ourselves imagining sexually perverse situations, for example, our animal intention (the intention of the intention) is the driving force. This intention of the intention is then screened by our intention as an individual. We can decide whether or not to allow the animal impulse to become the impulse of an individual. Once our impulse as an individual has been decided, only then do we decide whether we will put it into practice. Notably, not thinking of putting a fantasy into practice is a behavior deriving from the individual impulse, despite the fact that it is the animal impulse that motivates it.

What is important in a relationship—what leads to feuds or to admiration—has to do with the intention of the individual, not the animal intention. The fool confuses the two and sees, in the light of human reactions and behavior, only the *yetzer ha-ra* (animal impulse), pure and undifferentiated. But this tells us nothing about an individual, only about all of us collectively. To judge someone for his animal spontaneity is to incur judgment upon oneself.

As we perceive that others relate to us while having to deal with their animal impulses (originating in a self-centered universe, aiming exclusively for survival), we can appreciate the true intentions and attitudes of others. Only in recognizing the *yetzer ha-ra* dimension, that of animal impulses, can we allow ourselves to like an enemy, as we will now see.

Opening Space (*Farginen*): The Antonym of Envy

Yiddish has a very special verb, unknown to most other languages: *farginen*. It means to open space, to share pleasure; it is the exact opposite of the verb *to envy*. While envy means disliking or resenting the happiness of others, *farginen* means making a pact with another individual's pleasure or happiness. This unique word represents the space in which we allow others to express their happiness, feeling of success, or gladness.

When a person shares the news that he has come into a lot of money, he often has to contend with forced smiles, with muttered and mumbled congratulations. These are verbal attempts at covering up envy, the difficulty people have in dealing with good things that happen to someone else.

At such times it is hard to avoid averting one's gaze and escaping within, to silent tormenting thoughts.

As if in a movie, one hears oneself repeating, in slow motion, "How wonderful, how nice," while questions echo inside, such as, "Why him? What I couldn't do with that much money. . . ." Usually in these situations, the difficulty in dealing with another's happiness is so obvious that the other person perceives it. Many friendships and confidences end in these rapid exchanges, when the worst and often unspoken fears about a friend are confirmed, with very little margin for error.

Though the envy felt at these destructive moments is real, this doesn't necessarily mean that evil is wished on the person whose happiness is so difficult to share. But sadly, the incident carries deep implications, and any positive goodwill that may exist in the relationship is immediately lost. So it is extremely important to be able to *fargint* another person.

Discipline is needed for *farginen*, because this feeling is rarely natural to human beings in their animal dimension. There is nothing wrong or false about seeking such learning. Like any other kind of social ability, such as not stealing, *farginen* comes through discipline. Perhaps the biggest misconception regarding this type of sentiment is to think that the gut or instinctive feeling is what indicates another person's sincerity about opening or not opening space for *farginen*. With *farginen*, just as with the dangers of seeing (discussed above), we must not get hung up on the level of the intention of the intention, but must still perceive the other's true intention. This is because we do not truly perceive the other's animal dimension. Actually, we love the other, care about him, and feel friendship for him because of his *divine* aspects—that is, the potential he has to develop himself and which pleases us, makes us feel tenderness, or speaks to our inner selves. Many times we can even love another individual's ability to *not* assimilate study and discipline, to remain spontaneous and instinctive, retaining part of his natural ingenuousness. But this is still an expression of spontaneity from someone who has successfully integrated aspects of his animal spontaneity into his divine self. We truly admire others who can grow, who transform themselves on the basis of their experience and culture, integrating (and not denying) their animal spontaneity.

Thus, when we are able to *farginen* someone spontaneously, it means we have done the required groundwork of dealing with our self-esteem, at least to some extent. But we will always have to work at reacting to opportunities for *farginen*, so as not to miss them.

To develop the ability to *farginen*, we must first recall from our own experience those moments when we were able to do it. And if this feeling was sincere, it will certainly have been felt with great happiness, a kind of catharsis. To reach *farginen* is an experience of freedom, in which we find ourselves liberated from the heavy load dragged by those who envy. This is a liberation from the fantasy that we can control the world around us: the very special feeling of not being limited to the sphere of the ego and individual consciousness. In fact, the utopia idealized by those who anticipate the creation of a messianic age—an era of understanding—is made up of people who live the feeling of *farginen* as easily as we, in our unredeemed world, feel envy.

Discipline is a fundamental factor. The greater the investment in life, the greater value given to the inner self, the easier it is to feel content with one's share in life. And the greater the satisfaction with life, the greater the ability to feel happy, to *farginen* other people. Every time we are able to celebrate someone else's happiness, we will, by definition, have greater reason to celebrate ourselves. In this way, we can widen our chances for enjoying life, freeing ourselves from the imprisonment of our own luck. *Farginen* sets up networks of confidence that enrich life.

It's much easier to suffer with a friend, to help someone who is less fortunate, than to *farginen*. It's much harder to sincerely share others' happiness. And the consequences are proportional: those whose suffering we share are eternally grateful, while those whose happiness we share will eternally care for us, as true friends.

Knowing How to Rebuke

> He who cannot accept correction shall certainly die before his time.
>
> —*Rabbi Naḥman of Bratslav*

Knowing how to correct or rebuke those around us is crucial to deflecting rancor and preventing conflict. Often, we imagine just the opposite: that we can avoid strife by keeping quiet and staying out of difficult situations. But this idea is quite mistaken. Even the Bible juxtaposes, in the same verse (Leviticus 19:17), the sentence "Do not hate your brother in your heart" with the conclusion "Certainly you shall rebuke your neighbor and not suffer sin upon him." The implication is obvious: when we don't criticize, we hate the other in our hearts, even if unconsciously. Such hatred plants the seed for the development of a feud.

Feuds seem to feed on the heart's acidity and bitterness, so they do not occur when there is absolute frankness. Those who do constant maintenance work on the heart, removing its acidity, are able to neutralize many opportunities for conflict, because they are utilizing their emotional and spiritual immune systems. This is a spiritual, somatic reality. The neglect of spiritual health leads to the development of emotional and affective difficulties. Criticizing others effectively is the best means for the removal of acidity from the heart.

The biblical text in question is not a pedagogical recommendation. It does not mean we should help others to perfect themselves. It is about creating an internal posture regarding misunderstandings and conflict. The heart, like any living organism, needs a balanced flow. When we allow feelings to remain blocked inside the heart, we suffer from a form of obesity, of retention.

Everyone has felt this. Perhaps from a sincere, constructive motivation we have at times tried to correct another person. Because correction is not easily carried out, such efforts often end badly. But when we take on certain internal postures, we are able to correct others constructively, encouraging encounters through discord that would not be possible if limited by a search for agreement or acceptance.

To criticize correctly, the Besht (the Baal Shem Tov, the eighteenth-century founder of Hasidism) recommends:

> When someone sees defects in another person and comes to dislike him because of these weaknesses, he himself certainly possesses something of these same defects. Thus, criticize yourself first for seeing defects, and only then, being in a state of relative impurity, criticize the other. In this way, you will not hate the other, but will care about him. When you criticize him, this will spring from an atmosphere of caring. In this way, the person will take kindly to you, linking what is good in himself with what is good in you.

The Besht suggests the transformation of discord that is not for the sake of Heaven into a discord that is. How do we do this? By merely realizing that discord comes from discontent that produces certainty and arrogance about the position we have taken. If we can empty our discord of the envious desire to prove another person wrong, if we instead enter a partnership over the disagreement, understanding it as an opportunity for both parties' personal growth, we turn that discord into something positive. In this way, we connect the good in others to the good in ourselves.

If we turn to a neighbor with a severe criticism that does not take into account our own humanity and our animal spontaneity, we bring up what is false and bad in ourselves. Of course, we will be greeted in turn with the other's inability to recognize his or her own animal spontaneity. When this happens, neither the person doing the criticizing is "himself because he is himself," nor is his object "himself because he is himself"; in other words, there is no dialogue. Only when we take on a critical perspective from the stance of knowing who we really are can we open channels of communication (including discord) for the sake of Heaven.

So, knowing how to criticize means we have to know how to analyze two questions. The first, as we saw, is whether or not we can enter into discord with integrity, "I being I because I am I." The second is whether or not the other party is in a corresponding situation, if "he is he because he is he." If this is not the case, we must give up on the criticism. Understanding this prevents many of the bad experiences we have with reproving other people and which often lead us to avoid taking stands. Rabbi Meir eloquently illustrates this issue:

> When the rabbis of Zanz and Sadigur began a rivalry, many disciples took sides. Rabbi Meir then read them a parable from *Yalkut*:
>> Once, a lion decided not to seek food until his breath was sweeter. He found a mule and said

to him, "Put your head near my mouth and tell me if my breath is sweet." The mule did so and responded negatively.

"How dare he insult me?" exclaimed the king of beasts and immediately devoured the mule.

Some days later, the lion met up with a wolf and put the same question to him. The wolf answered in the affirmative. "How dare you lie to me?" roared the lion, and devoured him at once.

Some time later, he questioned a fox, an animal that does not let himself get mixed up in complicated situations. "Excuse me," said the fox. "I have a cold and have lost my sense of smell."

"Get yourselves a cold as well," said Rabbi Meir to his disciples, "and you will also be saved from the lion."

Knowing when another is unprepared to participate in discord for the sake of Heaven is fundamental. Even when one person is well intentioned, he may not necessarily find something good in the other to link up with. In such cases, we are obliged to remove ourselves from discord and to perceive ourselves as adults in relation to babies who don't know how to walk. Our responsibility is of another kind, and that being the case, we safeguard our hearts from unnecessary retention of rancor.

Thus we should be wise in reproving others, knowing when to do so and when not to. Rabbi Naḥman of

Bratslav sums up the prescription: "Be wise in your criticism, or you will do more evil than good." And he adds the following comments:

> Include yourself in any criticism you may make. Criticism that is held back destroys the chances of mercy, indulgence, and benevolence.
> Criticism brings from Heaven contentment and blessings.

No More Mr. Nice Guy

People often end up attracting rancor because they are constantly trying to be "nice." When we're obsessed with justifying and explaining our every act, we eliminate certain opportunities for dialogue.

An American educator was once traveling with his adolescent son. The son contested everything the father said. The father, knowing all about teenagers' needs, immediately understood what was happening and accepted his son's contrariness. Since this attitude did not satisfy the son and actually increased his irritability, the father realized that the son did not want to be understood; he in fact wanted a confrontation. He needed to mark out his territory and define his personality, to be different from his father. As long as the father did not understand that his role was to be "mean," and that the most practical attitude would be to allow his son to judge him—and not as a particularly wonderful person—he was unable to prevent the gap between them from widening.

Many times we must not be "nice," so as to open the way for others to see us as "mean." Many parents deepen misunderstandings with their children because they cannot accept themselves as being "not nice" in other people's eyes. Often, others need to see our weaknesses and doubts in order to perceive us as less threatening. Not being nice does not mean being wrong or evil, but opening up space for those who, faced with an authority figure, need to affirm themselves. Realizing this isn't easy, because not being nice implies a black mark on one's self-image.

A person who allows himself to be not nice at the right moment can deflect much rancor directed toward him, exactly because of what this symbolizes for others. Here is a story about it:

> The wife of Rebbe Yaakov Yitzḥak (the Yahudi) was very ill-tempered and often argued with him. The Yahudi never allowed himself to be provoked, never answered back with even one word. But once, his wife bothered him more than usual and he answered her with a few words. Rabbi Bunam asked him, "Why did you abandon your old habit of not answering back?"
>
> "Because I realized that what bothered my wife most was the fact that I didn't care about her complaints," answered the Yahudi. "The words I used with her actually represent an act of caring."

The Yahudi had chosen to come down from the heights of his wisdom and become involved in a mundane discussion, because he knew that the dignified posture that he maintained as an elder could not open new opportunities for relationship and dialogue. He realized that playing the role of a mean person with a prosaic and vulgar attitude was the wisest course of action in this case.

Being not nice is a price paid by those who hold positions of prominence. Any leader who wants to retain his charisma must know when to accept criticism, even if he could easily defend himself against it. Criticism is often the mirror image of success, of being important and well liked. One does not come without the other. A particular criticism may be nothing more than a means to legitimate the act of criticizing. People often deflect criticism, arduously defending themselves, when all they really need to do to deflate a critic is merely recognize his right to criticize. This is about recognizing that no one is perfect, and that no matter how well we hide our faults, some criticism will be pertinent. Once this has been proven, a critic will cease his exhaustive efforts. Those who don't permit a realignment of relationships, who insist on being right and good, never reaffirming their humility, will be implacably persecuted. The Rabbi of Ropshitz commented:

> Moses lived his life as a recluse and set up his tent outside the campsite. As a result, his critics accused him of being exclusive and indifferent.

Aaron, on the other hand, went to the trouble of pacifying those who argued and was always moving among the people in the campsite. Aaron was criticized for being too democratic and failing to give himself the respect due to his position of honor. The opponents of an important man will condemn him, no matter what his behavior!

Once this is known, a leader may not always have to answer his critics. If he knows how to absorb them, by being not nice, his popularity will certainly increase. This is because being nice takes up a great deal of space and, as we have seen, leads to having your foot stepped on.

Thus there are times when allowing ourselves to be criticized, instead of becoming defensive and self-justifying, can be an effective tool in a feud. Even an adversary, hearing bad things said about you, will let down his guard and become more willing to reconsider his position than he would if he had heard only words of praise and exaltation. We need to know how to live with the fact that others may make negative comments about us.

It is told that once the Besht said to his disciples, "Go and meet with the Sacred Gaon Rabbi Isaac, and speak badly about me to him."

The disciples looked at him in surprise.

Then he revealed, "Do this so that the great rabbi may find satisfaction and his heart become glad."

Knowing how to live with not being nice is fundamental, in order to dissipate the residues of envy that even the wise find difficult to neutralize. These residues are not objective; many times the envy is not even directed at us. But once we invest in the nice-guy role, it are immediately mobilized against us.

Living with Ill Will

Ill will is one of the biggest factors in feuds and acts of revenge. In the early chapters of this book we saw that a refusal to lend someone something, for example, generates small incidents involving humiliation, which are taken personally and set off arrogance, which is answered with pride, and so on. The result of this chain reaction is the start of a feud.

Here we will observe how to avoid a feud, by knowing the rights of each party involved in a conflict, especially the right to withhold goodwill. A story in the Talmud (*Bava Batra* 7a) illustrates the perfect situation for our analysis of ill will:

> Once, a man began building a wall in front of his neighbor's window. The neighbor protested, "You are blocking the light from my house."
>
> The man responded, "I will seal up your window and make another one for you, above the level of my wall."
>
> "No," said the neighbor, "you'll spoil my wall if you do that."

"In that case," said the man, "I'll knock down your wall and rebuild it with a window higher than my wall."

"No, never," the neighbor quickly replied. "One new wall in an old house won't be very firm."

"In that case," said the man, "Let me demolish the whole house and rebuild it with windows above the level of my wall."

"And where will I live during the construction period?" said the neighbor pensively.

"I'll rent a house for you during that time," said the man.

"Ah . . . no. I don't want to take the trouble," sighed the neighbor.

Rabbi Ḥama said, "The neighbor has every legal right to prevent the wall from being built."

The neighbor has no obligation to "take the trouble." Understanding this principle is fundamental, because it allows us to visualize the situation from another person's point of view. Changing angles, what appeared to be "ill will" becomes "imposed will." No one has to leave his house, move his belongings, reorganize himself in new surroundings, and so on, just because someone wants to build a wall. The sequence of examples in the Talmud could actually go on and on, with promises to move furniture, install the neighbor elsewhere, et cetera, and even so, he would have the prerogative to prefer not to "take the trouble."

Much goodwill and wisdom are needed to avoid

perceiving the neighbor's attitude as ill will. This is very difficult, and so these situations often lead to hatred and envy. We keep thinking, "I did everything I could to accommodate the guy, but he didn't want to help out. What's his problem?" The real issue is that no one can calculate the cost of such a favor to someone else. No one can measure the trouble that moving would have caused the neighbor. His peculiarities and idiosyncrasies are not necessarily the same as those of the man who is pressuring him to accept the wall. This is why the latter cannot judge his neighbor, to discover whether his motivation was in fact ill will or merely a question of convenience.

When we ask to borrow something, we should always be alert, because we are unable to evaluate whether or not a refusal is motivated by pettiness. We can compare situations of mutual lending and then consider notions of ill will, revenge, or feuding, as we saw earlier. But, from a unilateral perspective, we cannot judge the importance or esteem a person gives to a thing.

Instead of getting angry when someone refuses to lend something, it helps to understand that although the loan would apparently be no effort on the part of the lender, this may not be his perception, and that his perception is as valid as that of the would-be borrower. The impulse to define another individual as an egotist can lead to great irony. It may in fact be the borrower who is the real egotist, unable to recognize the costs or inconvenience that a loan may represent. The facile conclusion that the favor involves little sacrifice actually attests to the would-be borrower's inability to drop his own assumptions and recognize another person's rights. Such behavior demonstrates a self-centered attitude.

We must recognize that working with the phrase "Love your neighbor as yourself" is very difficult, because we ourselves are also the "neighbor."

We Are Also the Neighbor: The Limits and Paradoxes of Loving Others As We Do Ourselves

In the section on ill will, we saw that we have the right to think of ourselves as the "other." Whether or not we wish to be generous, we recognize that altruism is not an obligation. When we expect others to be generous, as if it were our right, we are in fact exposing our own egotism. Actually, we end up confused in the attempt to set up criteria to define the "other," our neighbor.

Obviously, we must love ourselves in order to love a neighbor as we do ourselves. But most of the interactions we have with others bring tensions and conflict that are part of living with other people, part of survival. In these cases, how can we love a neighbor as we would ourselves? If during a dispute we love the other as we do ourselves, we end up loving ourselves less, and thus we lack the self-love required for loving the neighbor. It is almost as if, in a dispute, we were called upon to love our neighbor *more* than we love ourselves. This is a constant contradiction, in everyday relations with others and in the way market economics function.

For centuries, a talmudic story (*Bava Metzia* 62a) has stimulated the imagination of commentators, helping us to clear up several points on this issue:

> Two men were traveling through the desert, and one of them carried a flask of water. If both drank the water, both would die. But if only one drank, he would be able to return to civilization.
>
> Ben Petura taught that in this case, both should drink and die, instead of one witnessing the other's death.
>
> Thus it was, until Rabbi Akiva came and taught, "It is written: 'And your brother shall live with you.' Meaning that your life comes before the life of your neighbor."

This story created a precedent that concerned many scholars. Rabbi Akiva's opinion is valid in terms of both theory and practice. After all, in times of mortal danger one's first concern is physical integrity. Both logic and instinct justify this behavior; until the best path of action is determined, the ability to act must be ensured, which depends exclusively on being alive. The problem in our story is a premeditated choice which clearly gives priority to one's own life over that of a neighbor.

Ahad ha-Am, a nineteenth-century Jewish thinker, sought to clarify this question:

Ben Petura, the altruist, does not value life for itself; for him it is better that two lives perish when death wants no more than one, just so that altruism can prevail. But Jewish morality looks at the question from a frontal, objective viewpoint. Every act that leads to the loss of life is vile by nature, even if it begins in the purest sentiments of love and compassion and even when the victim is the agent of his own death. In the case before us, when it is possible to save one of the two lives, there is a moral obligation to overcome the feelings of compassion and save what can be saved. But whom to save? Justice answers: he who has the means to save himself! The life of each human being is entrusted to each one to safeguard, and fulfilling this duty is a more important obligation than saving one's neighbor.

Notably, this is a hypothetical situation about safeguarding one's own life, to the exclusion of moral complications. The ethical issues regarding others' lives go beyond the case at hand. The Talmud, for example, is clear and categorical in the following situation: if you are sent to kill a person under penalty of losing your own life, you must pay with your own life and refuse to obey the order. The Talmud gives the reason for this in the form of a question: "Who says your blood is more crimson than your neighbor's?" What is difficult about this case is that we are dealing not with external values as they influence a situation, but with the indifferent violence of the desert. Thus we have a threshold situation about the value of one's own life as compared with that of another person.

We should also recognize that while Rabbi Akiva's position seems to make good sense, it is difficult to understand how the phrase "Love your neighbor as yourself" can be put into practice, because any important situation that puts us in opposition to another individual is vulnerable to his logic. We would then be instituting, in practice, the phrase "Let's love our neighbor less than ourselves." Professor Louis Jacobs takes the question further:

> Even if Rabbi Akiva's opinion is adopted, it should not be interpreted solely as if he were teaching that there is no moral obligation for both to die, if one person can drink the water and survive. It means, simply, that the one who has the water can drink it, but this is very different from what Achad Ha-Am said about the issue, i.e., that "fulfilling the duty [of safeguarding one life] is a nearer obligation than preserving the life of one's neighbor." The question is simply that there is no obligation to give water to the other man, since, in this case, he should also return it! Rabbi Akiva would agree, however, that if the man who has the water wanted to give it to his companion, this would be a very special and pious attitude. . . . Ben Petura would also make no objection to one of the parties passing the water to the other so he could survive. The debate between Rabbi Akiva and Ben Petura is only about the situation in

which both want to drink the water; in this case, Akiva argues that it would be wrong for both to perish, if one could be saved. . . . However, the rare individual who in a moment of great crisis could rise to the point of giving his life for another's . . . is considered a just man, and would be recognized as such by Judaism.

This case parallels the idea of ill will. We have a right to ill will, although this may not be an ideal or exemplary attitude. Loving others as we would ourselves is a very radical precept, which, on the one hand, serves as a structural model for a utopian world and, on the other, does not aid in the mediation between an individual's ideals and this unredeemed, imperfect world. We will soon see that some attempts to humanize this phrase and turn it into something more than a fictional, futuristic museum piece may come up with a more active role for it in the transformation of the world.

The apparent paradox contained in this phrase is represented in the talmudic statement that we are also the "other." We have the right to love ourselves in our capacity as neighbor, and this will certainly assure us a right to look out for own survival. One last story, however, should open our eyes to the frontiers we are exploring, and to how each moment in each situation can, no matter how small the detail involved, totally change an issue's ethical perspective.

The story is about Rabbi Baruch son of Rabbi Ḥayyim of Zanz, who was traveling to Gorletz on a terribly cold day, wrapped in a bearskin. One of his traveling companions didn't even have a coat and, suffering desperately from the cold, took ill and came close to death. When Rabbi Ḥayyim heard this, he gave his son a severe scolding, anxiously asking, "Why didn't you give him your bearskin?"

Rabbi Baruch replied, "Father, I had only one skin!"

"You should have given it anyway, " said Rabbi Ḥayyim.

Rabbi Shlomo of Radomsk, hearing the discussion, interrupted, "So you prefer to put your own son's life at risk, even though it is written [in the Talmud], 'Anyone is like your own neighbor . . . each one is like his neighbor.' "

"That is true without a doubt," said Rabbi Ḥayyim, "but you must know, Rabbi, that when a question of life and death arises, we do not need to proceed exactly in accordance with what is written."

Our paradox can only be solved when we recognize that an acquired right, regarding extremely important questions, does not necessarily lead to the correct behavior. Between right and wrong, a universe exists where every human being molds his own face, or his mask. Knowing what is not wrong is only part of an effort to get to what is right. What is written, the Law, is not a manual of what is right, but of what is wrong or not wrong.

To understand the dimension of what is right, we should not devote ourselves to the effort of searching for what is wrong, but should constantly invest in the study of law and personal growth. Law is to be understood here as the ability to envision the larger picture, and personal growth as an ever-changing and challenging comprehension of our perception of ourselves and of reality. In this sense, the phrase "Love your neighbor as yourself" leaves something to be desired. As the rabbis warn us, it influences our world from the future. For the rabbis, the future interferes in the present as well as the past, and this phrase dreamt in the past, from our future, also makes itself perceptible in the present. Later we will look at some ideas about dealing with the anachronism of this phrase.

Counting the Costs of Conflict

This happens in every bad business deal: we make detailed calculations of every possible source of profit, but when it comes to adding up the costs, we relax. For the same reason, many conflicts that we get into turn out to be bad deals. Thus hatred, in inciting conflict with total irresponsibility, becomes a terribly unreliable business partner.

The crux of a feud or long-standing disagreement is our imprisonment by the other. Although we rarely permit ourselves to realize it, hating someone is in fact a form of dependence. By hating, we create a situation in which we grant enormous power over ourselves to the person we hate. In this respect, Jewish tradition cautions us to take great care with the roles we allow others to play in our lives. Once we give the object of our hatred access to our imagination, we give him or her the right to be linked to our lives, and we end up sharing a common future. As with a marriage or love affair, once we dive into the relationship with determined intensity, we must be aware that we have involved another person and created responsibilities for him or her.

Thus, if someone evokes repulsion or hatred in you, and you really want to stay as far away as possible from this person, the best solution is not to hate him. If you allow yourself to fall into the trap of rancor, and especially the trap of feuding, you will acquire the unhappy experience of bringing the person you hate very close to yourself.

The basic issue is whom we allow to create ties with us, at our own initiative, and whether we are aware of the involvement we thus enter into. We must pay attention to the fact that becoming involved (by hating) sets up responsibilities from which we cannot escape alone, under penalty of suffering from guilt and a conscience tormented by the thought that we might not have acted correctly. The Rabbi of Amshinov makes a simple and concise commentary:

> To do evil to another person is worse than doing evil to the Creator. The person you harmed may have gone someplace unknown to you, and you

will have then lost the chance to ask his forgiveness. The Eternal One, however, is everywhere, and you can find Him anytime you seek Him.

Every time we harm a person, even in word or thought, we become slaves of a situation in which that person is the only one who can free us. Do we want this? In the Talmud (*Taanit* 20a), we find a surprising story of the level of commitment we can involuntarily take on by giving in to our rancorous impulses:

Once, Rabbi Eleazar left the city of Gedor, where his master lived, to return home. Mounted on a donkey, traveling a riverbank, pleased and proud of the teachings he had received from his master, he met an extremely ugly man.

"Peace be with you, my lord," said the man.

Rabbi Eleazar in turn replied, "Oh! Might the people of the town where you live all be so . . . rustic as you?"

"This I cannot say," answered the man, "but maybe you should ask the Creator who shaped me, saying to Him: How ugly is this vessel You have created!"

Realizing that he had given offense, Rabbi Eleazar dismounted his donkey and prostrated himself before the man, saying, "I have committed a terrible offense against you. Forgive me!"

But the man refused and said, "I will not pardon you until you face the Creator who shaped me and say to Him: How ugly is this vessel You have created!"

Rabbi Eleazar did not want to leave him and walked with him until they came upon the town where Rabbi Eleazar lived. The people of the place, hearing that their master was returning, went out to greet him, saying, "Peace be with you, our rabbi, our master!" The ugly man, who preceded Rabbi Eleazar, asked the people whom they were addressing as "rabbi" and "master." They then pointed to Rabbi Eleazar.

The ugly man then said, "If he is a rabbi, may there not be many like him in Israel!"

"Why not?" the people asked, surprised.

He answered, "Because of the way he treated me." When they heard the story of what had happened, all the people rushed forward and implored, "Forgive him, as he is a great student of the Torah."

The ugly man then conceded, "Only for you will I forgive him, and only on condition that he never again repeat such behavior."

In this story, we find a careless attitude on the part of Rabbi Eleazar, who, ironically, was so delighted with what he had learned with his master. When the ugly man asks, "Who is the rabbi, the master?" we vividly perceive, having all experienced similar situations, how easy it is to fall victim to an inability to understand the dimension of our interactions and involvement with others.

Rabbi's Eleazar's desperation, illustrated by his following the offended man, shows us that he was aware of his error. The last thing he could do at that moment would be to lose sight of the ugly man, because he needed his forgiveness. He had become a slave to his own mistake. His impropriety turned him from a free man enjoying the return journey home, after a rich experience with his master, into a caricature, groveling in search of liberation. "Dismounting the donkey" is an attitude that we should take before getting involved in a situation that could lead to a feud. This phrase actually means counting the real costs of a conflict. It symbolizes the understanding that being happy and "up" does not keep us from making fools of ourselves. Haven't we all, like Rabbi Eleazar, had the experience of feeling so happy and sure of ourselves that we forgot about the serious care that relationships require? Who has not told a joke that set off a violent reaction and left us ashamed? Or acted insensitively and felt guilty later?

Jewish tradition believes that this kind of behavior can become a transcendental debt, with costs that are added up for payment, sooner or later. Any interaction demands great care. Even the simple attempt to gain forgiveness can greatly aggravate a dispute and increase its costs, because attaining to the equilibrium of pardon and remorse is not easy.

Very often during a misunderstanding, our pleas for forgiveness are not heeded, as is the case in the above story. Not everyone has a conscience like Rabbi Eleazar, who did not weaken in his attempt to solve the problem, despite the other man's refusal. In everyday situations, a denied request for forgiveness frequently brings about renewed resentment, for both parties. "You don't want to forgive me? Too bad for you. . . ." This is an example of a reaction that makes the aggressor feel humiliated, and the offended party even more angry, over the aborted attempt to restore justice. The costs in cases such as this one get bigger and bigger, reaching the astronomical sums of wasted energy that feuds can cause.

This is why, even when we aren't interested in paying the costs of a conflict, it is better to stay in one rather than begin a long and torturous search for forgiveness. Such a search can lead to an even more costly widening of the conflict, and ever greater involvement with the other party. Perhaps the story of the dispute between the Rabbi of Chernobyl and his adversary can shed some light on this phenomenon.

Rabbi Naḥum of Chernobyl had an opponent who often insulted him. This man gradually started to suffer losses in his business, and so he decided to seek ways to reconcile himself with the rabbi. When he asked the rabbi to forgive him, the former replied, "I pardon you in the same spirit with which you are asking me to pardon you."

But the business losses went on, and the disciples began to intervene, asking the rabbi to truly forgive the man from the bottom of his heart. The rabbi agreed, but the man began to lose more and more, faster and faster, until he was left without a cent. The disciples then asked the rabbi why his pardon had added even greater punishment to the man, and he answered:

"Moses was the most modest of men. When his sister insulted him, he did not take it badly and immediately forgave her. But God inflicted upon her an even greater punishment (Numbers 12:10). The same occurs with me. The deeper my pardon, the more severe is the divine punishment, because this man has not sincerely repented of his offenses from the bottom of his heart."

The Rabbi of Chernobyl knew that the more unbalanced the process of reconciliation, the greater the cost involved, at least for one of the two sides. He realized that sometimes it is better not to forgive, when the pardon represents a unilateral attitude. In other words, it may not be better to invest in great purity of feeling, when the other cannot reach the greatness of such behavior. Thus, one should seek peace in one's heart, without making external gestures of magnanimity or maturity. It may also be better for the aggressor to pay the costs of his insult than to get involved in an insincere process of reconciliation. This is because the true definition of a feud is in fact an imbalance of intentions. To cover this up in a false process will always deepen the disagreement, in one way or another.

A true pardon is a process of mutual responsibility. The offended party should want the aggressor to voice his regret, not only to cure the wounds of aggression, but for the aggressor's own benefit, so as to free himself of the burden he chose to take on. The reciprocal is also true: the aggressor should seek forgiveness not only in an expectation of redemption but, above all, so that the other can find peace in his heart.

The wisdom of seeking true reconciliation is really about managing the imbalance or disparity of intentions of the parties involved. Like weighing something on the scale, the more grandiose one person's show of feeling, the greater the tendency for the other to take on an opposite attitude, with immense costs. Note that the rabbi in the story, in acceding to his disciples' request, perhaps making a sacrifice in the name of pedagogical principles, also runs up certain costs. His act of magnanimity, which for obvious reasons he did not own up to from the start, increases his responsibility and his involvement in a feud, with the aggravating factor of this having caused his adversary's financial losses.

This is a very important notion. There can be no winner when our adversary suffers because of us. Even if the suffering derives from the behavior of the adversary himself, and we have nothing to do with its consequences, it will still have been our fault. Could we have reduced the disparity of intentions, if we had been wiser? Possibly. Thus we are also responsible (perhaps not totally without intent) for the seriousness of the consequences affecting the other.

The real lesson here is that interaction is a state of being. There is no exit from this state, unless there is a mutual attitude. The just person is not the one who purifies his heart and contrasts it to the "filth" of the other's, but rather the one who takes on responsibilities linked to the impurities of the other's heart.

Because interaction is a state beyond our control and puts us into partnership with another person's life, it is very important to correctly count the costs of any involvement, especially those meant to end conflicts and feuds.

Exercises against Irritation

Some behavioral exercises may help us to avoid hasty moves toward conflict. To do them, it is important to recognize that peace and perfect tranquillity are transitory states of equilibrium, and that instead of becoming irritated with their impermanence, one should simply try one's best to return to them as quickly as possible. Tranquillity may come with a hammock hung between two coconut trees, a splendid late afternoon, a drink and a favorite book, a relaxed mind and an empty schedule. But the hammock can grow uncomfortable, or an insect may intrude, illustrating the difficulty of finding equilibrium with the external world, which is always in flux.

One of the ways that we come closest to experiencing the diversity and the dynamic aspect of life is through the encounter with the "other." This other can violently interact with us, either physically or with an informal comment. For example, he may assault us or simply, just as we stretch out in the hammock, start talking to us from a distance, yet not loud enough for us to make out his words. The attention and effort required to respond to such a message directed to us is often totally unbearable.

To deal with this, we need to develop certain skills. Some are able to complete the course of this learning, emerging unharmed, while others are not. To caricature a classic image of Jewish mysticism,* we might speak of the four wise men who met in the orchard of hatred. One of them ended up with a terrible asthma attack; another with gastritis; another with high blood pressure, while only the fourth emerged unscathed. This last person had a particular internal posture and certainly made use of age-old secret techniques allowing him to taste the fruits of irritation and provocation, digesting them easily. Here are some of the rabbis' secret prescriptions to be remembered and used daily:

1. Become aware of the moment you are irritated.

> Reb Bunam said, citing a verse from the Scriptures, " 'Appoint yourselves judges and officers in all your gates . . . ' (Deuteronomy 16:18). This means first judge correctly how you should behave at your 'gates,' that is, your limbs and your

---

*One of the Talmud's most famous references to mystical speculation is the story of four sages who went on a spiritual journey through the "orchard of interpretation." By way of presenting the dangers of such an enterprise, the story tells us that only one of the four, Rabbi Akiva, emerged safely, while the others fell prey to heresy, madness, and death.

senses; only then make use of your officers to execute your judgments."

2. Do not be hasty.

The Rabbi of Gastinin cultivated the habit of never expressing his displeasure with someone on the day he was offended or disrespected by that person. On the following day, he would go to the person in question and say, "I was annoyed with you yesterday."

3. As you go out to begin your day, recognize the dynamic reality of interactions and prepare for them.

Once, the Rabbi of Vorka was traveling with a friend in a carriage. His companion complained that the coachman was going too fast. To this the coachman reacted in a violent manner, insulting both passengers.

"How can you be so calm and accept this abuse?" wondered the rabbi's traveling companion.

The rabbi answered, "Because I was prepared for even more insolence and abuse than that which we are receiving."

4. As a behavioral prescription for reducing external and internal discord, take the formula given in the commentaries known as *Pirkei Avot de-Rabbi Natan*:

> If you commit a small error regarding your neigh-
> bor, may this be taken as a very serious issue;
> but if you did a great favor for your neighbor, may
> this be taken as something insignificant, a trifle.
>
> And if your neighbor, for his part, did you a
> small favor, may this be something grandiose in
> your eyes; but if he did you great ill, may this be
> small in your eyes.

In other words, irritation and rage are phenomena
that tend to take on importance—or not—depending on
our initial expectation. Whoever wants to live with as
little unpleasantness as possible must work on his or
her expectations regarding others. These are daily exercises for avoiding disappointment, for being surprised.
They enable us not to demand what cannot be required
of others.

Obviously, each person's internal posture and maturity contribute to just how much "gastric irritation"
he or she suffers from passing through the orchard. But
in order not to fall victim to mere good intentions and
rhetoric, every initiate should first try to cultivate the
habit of doing the basic exercises.

In this sense, the great model of Jewish tradition
was the sage Hillel. His patience was legendary, and
his knowledge of the paths of irritation turned him into
a true master of his own life. A curious story in the
Talmud (*Sanhedrin* 7a) gives the wonderful example of
a conscious effort to avoid becoming irritated:

> Once, two men decided to bet four hundred *zuzim*
> on who could irritate the sage Hillel. One of them

decided, "I will be able to irritate him." On a Friday, as dusk fell, when Hillel was bathing [preparing for the Sabbath], this man appeared at the door of his house and shouted, "Does Hillel live here?"

Hillel wrapped himself in a robe and went to meet the man. "My son," he said, "what do you want?"

"I have a question to ask you," the man answered.

"You may ask, my son, you may ask," said Hillel.

"Why are the Babylonians' heads long?" he asked.

Hillel answered, "You have asked a good question, my son. It is because they do not have well-trained midwives."

The visitor left and soon returned, shouting, "Does Hillel live here?"

Hillel once more donned his robe and greeted him, "My son, what do you desire?"

"I have a question to ask you," said the man.

"Ask, my son, ask," replied Hillel.

"Why do people from Palmyra have poor eyesight?" asked the visitor.

Said Hillel, "You have asked a good question. It is because they live in a very sandy region, and their eyes are constantly irritated by the sand lifted up by the wind."

The man departed but returned once again, shouting, "Does Hillel live here?"

Hillel greeted his questioner once again, saying, "What do you desire, my son?"

"I have a question to ask you," said the man.

"Ask, my son, ask," repeated Hillel.

"Why are the Ethiopians' feet so big?" asked the visitor.

"You have asked a good question," said Hillel. "It is because they live on swampy terrain, and so it is easier for them to move about with big feet."

"I have many other questions," said the man, "but I am worried, because I think I will end up irritating you with them."

Hillel pulled up a bench and, sitting down, he said, "Please ask whatever questions you have."

The man then asked, "Are you by any chance Hillel, the one they call the Prince of Israel?"

"Yes," answered Hillel.

"If it is true, I pray there are not many like you in Israel," said the visitor.

Hillel then inquired, "Why, my son?"

To which the man replied, "Because it is your fault I have lost four hundred *zuzim* that I would have won if I had succeeded in irritating you!"

Hillel responded, "It is much better that you lose four hundred *zuzim* than that Hillel lose his patience."

Valuing patience and not selling it cheaply is a perception of the sage and of those who see.

Tuning In to Your Angels

As we saw in "Knowing How to Rebuke," rage must be kept in balance. Both too much and too little rage expressed to others will deepen conflict. Aristotle said twenty-five centuries ago: "Anyone may become angry—this is easy; but being angry with the right person, in the right proportion, at the right time, for the right reason, and in the right way—this is not in everyone's reach."

The rabbis recognized this, although they also believed that the failure to attain this "ideal anger" is due to an inability to utilize a very subtle aspect of human potential. "Right anger" is not a task for logic or the intellect, which is preoccupied with hierarchies and easy prey for the ego. Convincing the intellect to plot and get involved in vengeful acts is very easy. The brain also gets instinctively enthusiastic about maneuvers to prove one's superiority.

Where can we turn, then? To the heart? This is also very tied up with anger. Emotional wounds quickly blind the heart, which is subject to the intellect, which in turn answers to the ego. Ultimately, there is no feud that does not fully unite the mind and heart. The question thus persists.

According to the rabbis, the task of preventing feuds and conflicts should be passed on to our angels. What are these angels? They are extensions of the divine Superego, but unlike God, they have a more human perspective on reality. Thus, angels would be slightly humanized energies of God, able to represent and voice anxieties and arguments that would certainly irritate the Judge of Judges, or the Court of Courts. In other words, angels are external figures, creative principles that understand our humanity and are not shocked when we show our true colors or curse an adversary. Thus we can be more sincere with angels than we would be with the Creator, and in this way we can evolve by facing up wisely to our disagreements.

Obviously, the caricature of angels whispering advice into our ears is a theoretical model to explain certain subtle relationships with reality. They exist. They are like imaginary "others" who are not really others, but who act as intermediaries, allowing us to still observe the other from our own perspective. This way, the angel does not demand that we love our neighbor as we love ourselves, but argues with us in our attempt to find a solution.

This may all become clearer if we look at the angel structure the rabbis imagined to exist in human relations, especially those involving conflict.

According to the rabbis, we have four angels that balance each other out: one in front, one to the right side, another to the left side, and the last one behind us. The angel to the front is there to stop us, saying,

"Take it easy. . . . Wait, what's the hurry?" The one to the rear pushes us ahead, saying, "Face it. Have the courage to go for it; don't back out now." The one to our left, near the heart, says, "Forget it. Let it be." The one to the right says, "Remember, don't let it go by, because you have a memory!"

Tuning in to the impulses of "advance, retreat, remember, and forget" is fundamental to calibrating our reactions. These angels have to do with a certain instinct that is key to the human ability to act, both when we (apparently) react externally; and when we do nothing about a situation. Actually, we set off certain types of feuds because of internal passivity or aggressiveness: the former comes about when we do not sufficiently develop an emotional reaction, and the latter when we do not express our soul's position, repressing it instead. Feuds also occur when outward passivity or aggressiveness betray internal decisions. In all these situations there is a lack of coordination between our (internal) legislative and judiciary branches and our external executive branch.

The two angels at our sides that exert power over forgetting and remembering are part of the legislative branch—that is, ethical thought and justification for our reactions. The front and rear angels coordinate, based on the lateral stimuli, what ought to be done or not done. They aid in the execution of what we determine to be correct.

These angel pairs correspond to two dimensions of thought belonging to the same ethical order, although they also correspond to two different areas of behavior: intent and attitude. Each one of these pairs has its own good sense, which, when calibrated together, leads to a good posture, a posture that suits each particular individual.

This way, without rough edges or internal squabbles, we can guard against feuds, even if a decision is wrong. We may even be instructed or led to understand what other posture may be more appropriate; but there is no doubt that tuning in to the angels will allow a person to listen. This is because being balanced with the angels is the same as "being me because I am I." In cases where we meet an "other who is other because he is himself," dialogue will ensue.

In fact, the angels are emissaries who take us out of our solitude without incurring a loss of identity. If God were the mediator of our disagreements, there would be no dialogue. The "one" and the "other" would have to accept the absolute, and this is the end of differentiation, of life, and of Creation. But the angels set up real encounters that the heart and mind do not allow. Alone, the heart or the mind dehumanizes the "other," falling into the kind of relationship that Martin Buber classified as I-It. These are silent relationships, ruled by each individual's personal internal agenda, which, though they appear to create noise and movement, do not establish dialogue. This is the world of no-agreement, where discord for the sake of Heaven does not progress. In it, very little happens; its atmosphere is tedious and its inhabitants obese.

Tuning in to one's angels means adjusting our antennae to capture real presences in the space external to us. Many times, we are so taken by our own perception of reality that we lose contact with the world. This outer reality is only made perceptible to us in the perfect balance among what pushes us forward, what pulls us back, what makes us forget, and what makes us remember. In the perfect tuning of these impulses, we allow ourselves to be in touch with the outside world, and "someone who is someone" can communicate with us.

Using Anatomy in Conflict

When a human being finds himself in a state of conflict, he instinctively readies his anatomy. Legs tense for running, fists close, eyes narrow on alert, and even the tongue and nerves put themselves at adrenaline's command.

Might there be some anatomical development that could promote peace, that could be used to avoid conflict? The rabbis say yes.

First, their analysis of the anatomical reality of mouth and ears points to several teachings. One mouth and two ears certainly express the concept of listening more and speaking less. And the capacity of the ears to hear on two sides is less binding than that of the mouth, whose emission is centered and taken as the definitive position of the person speaking. Still, the ears are the source of many misunderstandings, so we must know how to use them in all their potential. The following discussion in the Talmud (*Ketubah* 5a) is important:

> Bar Kappara said, "If a person hears something improper, he should put his fingers in his ears." This is what Rabbi Eleazar meant when he asked rhetorically, "Why are a person's fingers tapered and conical at the tips?" Might he be asking why the fingers are separated from each other? Not at all! They are separated because each one has a different function. Thus, we must infer that he was asking exactly why fingers are tapered and conical. The answer is clear: so that upon hearing something improper, we may put our fingers in our ears.
>
> At the school of Ishmael, it was taught that the ear is rigid, while the earlobe is flexible and soft. Why? So that when hearing something improper, we may cover the ear cavity with the earlobe.

Using one's ears well does not simply mean listening, but above all knowing when not to listen. Knowing how to listen is a much more complicated task than putting the eardrums to work (as is the task of seeing, discussed earlier). Knowing how to listen to what others say, knowing when it is our duty to listen, knowing how to coordinate the mouth with the ears, so as to listen without allowing leakage through the oral orifice—these examples demonstrate the responsibility implied in the act of listening. If you did not hear well, conclude nothing; wait for other messages, by way of other senses, to confirm the aural message.

While the mouth is the organ through which the ears may leak, the tongue is more independent. The rabbis compared it, in much of its activity, to a snake. Lacking rigid bones, the tongue wanders around the mouth awaiting an opportunity and a prey. In its crawling, the tongue must be tamed. Some mystics believe that Moses chose to be tongue-tied and that this speech defect was key to his great and long leadership.

Rhetoric is one of the most dangerous practices, because when the tongue-serpent is totally free, as it engages in blah-blah-blah, it ends up contaminating the mouth and the person who owns it. Poisoned by discourse, the person is unlikely to recover.

How can the tongue be tamed? "Teach your tongue to say, 'I don't know!'; else you will be caught saying foolishness" (*Berakhot* 4a). The tongue should learn to say only two negatives: "no" and "I don't know." It is the tongue's job to say no so that the heart won't have to undertake responsibility for this task, for which it is not adequately prepared.

It is also the good tongue's work to say "I don't know," a task that should never be passed on to the ego or the intellect. On the other hand, the functions of "yes" and "I know" ought to be in the domain of the heart and the intellect, respectively. In other words, training the tongue is a civilizing act, similar to the way we train the sphincter. Those who know how to deal with their tongues are the ones who can train them to the point of being able to silence them quickly in a moment of excitement. Rabbi Ulla said, "Of two people who are fighting, the one who falls silent first is the most admirable."

The eyes are also important. Earlier, we looked at some aspects of seeing well. But the anatomy can also teach us much. For example, like ears, eyes also come in pairs, meant to compose a real image that is neither what one nor the other side sees. In this sense also, the eyelids are very important, for they permit us to not see. Not seeing is as essential as not hearing, and is responsible for building much that is positive in this world.

Should we adopt, as a human ideal, the mystical vision of the fish, whose eyes never close? Never! Note that the world of fish is one in which one individual swallows another. Of course, the contrary appears to be true—that justice and fairness would reign in the world of those who can see all. However, only the Creator can undertake this unimaginable feat of seeing all without becoming violent and vengeful. Only a being that is compassionate by design can keep its eyes open all the time. Neither we nor the fish are made of this structure.

Our compassion comes from the act of not seeing at certain moments. As the Eternal One forgets nothing, we need to forget so that we can be constructive; we need blindness to see better what the eyes, structurally speaking, do not wish to see. This is why we darken a room when meditating, and travel among the dreams of the unconscious, in the darkness of sleep.

Who among us could bear the world we live in if we could see it, focus on it, totally free from the veils that protect us? If not for the eyelids, we would be bitter, unconstructive souls. A talmudic story reveals this idea. Rabbi Yoḥanan ben Zakkai, a famous rabbi from the first century, to whom many mystical teachings are attributed, had to hide with his son to flee the Roman prohibition against the study of the Scriptures and tradition. They hid in a cave for fourteen years, sunk in mud to the waist, dedicating themselves only to study. When they finally emerged from the cave, purified and viewing everything through the eyes of wisdom, they perceived a hostile and unjust world. Their indignation and the power acquired from study caused everything they looked at in this world to be immediately destroyed. Their vision became so open, so critical, that they could not bear the reality of this world. The divine Voice had to intercede, to stop them: "What are you doing? You will destroy My world. . . . Back to the cave!"

Absolute vision is lethal in the dimension of life. Of course, by not seeing we permit the existence of horrible things, of injustices that we have not faced up to. But for those who see in the dark, not seeing does not mean no-vision. A person may close his eyes and try to not-see, so that he may have true insight. Thus he recognizes the hidden temptations to justice that incite us to destruction.

This is, for example, the function of saliva: to constantly remind us that we must learn to swallow. The building of this world, of a new era or of the messianic age, we owe to innumerable heroes who knew how to swallow when it was necessary. Imagine the courage and daring of those who managed this feat. The monuments of the future will be erected to them, replacing generals, politicians, and those who sought revenge. They will be statues of those who knew how to resist the temptation to undertake what was not theirs to do; who knew how to lose in order to make true conquest possible.

Banking on Being Naive

We have spoken about the great anonymous heroes who bravely persisted in preserving a space for faith and confidence in our world. In the Talmud (*Eduyyot*, 9b) there is a relevant story:

> Akavyah ben Mahalalel disagreed with his rabbinic colleagues on four different questions relating to the law. The sages asked him to abandon his position, promising him that he would be given the post of President of the Judges. He responded by saying, "I would rather be called a fool by humans than be evil in the eyes of God."

This is an extremely important idea. It is better to bank on one's internal belief, one's ingenuousness, than to accede to a need for recognition and acceptance by others. The spectrum of this notion is so wide that it exposes the individual to battles of values versus opportunity, or even belief versus survival. This attitude points up the readiness to sacrifice the well-being of the body for that of the soul. It contains in it the concept of martyrdom.

Martyrs, no matter how great or small their cause, affect us deeply, precisely because we find their tendency in ourselves. We discover, without understanding very well, that we are capable of acting in a disconnected manner in relation to the objective world of nature and survival, in the name of very subjective things. Like instinctively suicidal whales that throw themselves up on the beach, astonishing their human witnesses, we find similarly strange natural impulses within ourselves.

Perhaps we should look at this behavior a bit more closely. A story by the famous Nobelist Isaac Bashevis Singer is helpful. "Gimpel the Fool" tells the story of an apparent simpleton who is constantly fooled, manipulated, and deceived by those around him. At work, he is made a fool of, and believes the most lame excuses. As if he were possessed by an inability to perceive or do evil, Gimpel's world includes a wife who constantly cheats on him. No matter how obvious this is (even his children are not his own, but fruits of her adultery), he accepts explanations that even the most mediocre individual would find incredible. The story brings the reader to the edge of his chair, indignant that Gimpel could be so humiliated and stepped on and yet remain so impassive, content with whatever is told him.

When he finds his wife in bed with another man, the latter tells him that although they are both naked, they were just looking for a lost object. Gimpel once again accepts the explanation, in good faith. Only at the end of the story, after his ingenuousness has apparently disgraced him and his wife has kicked him out of the house, does Gimpel reveal his true dimensions. He goes out into the world, becomes a famous writer, and turns into a person of great clarity and vision. The author quickly reverses the reader's perception, revealing Gimpel's family and their world as the real fools. Every time they laughed at Gimpel's naiveté and the way he let himself be fooled, they were really laughing at themselves and the way they allowed themselves to be fooled.

There are moments in our lives when we must pay the costs of appearing foolish to others, to protect our souls and our dignity. In the world we live in, a person who allows himself to believe others, to deal with others as if they were innocent, and not malicious, until proven otherwise, is the object of ridicule. "You fell for that one? I don't believe it!" These and other such interjections are initiations to which all of us have been exposed, meant to strip us of our ingenuousness.

And what is ingenuousness for? It is a source of antibodies against intrigue, gossip, rancor, and the predisposition to taking things personally. The less naive we are, the more susceptible we are to feuding. It is as if we have become diabetics, with a total intolerance for sweets—as if we don't produce enough insulin to process true sweetness in other people.

It is incredible to think that Singer wrote this story in the midst of World War II, in 1944, when the first stories of the concentration camps were reaching America. It is quite probable that Gimpel symbolized the heroes who would later be seen as lambs going to slaughter. The passivity of the exterminated Jews, Gypsies, and homosexuals caused astonishment. Was it possible that these people did not see, did not realize what was going on?

Perhaps not. Maybe in the face of a hideous situation, blind faith is a legitimate human reaction. Note that this behavior borders on alienation, a disconnection from reality. Because the difference between foolishness and naiveté is so subtle, the latter often escapes us, absorbed as we are in the wish to avoid playing the fool.

Obviously, ingenuousness is dangerous to survival, just like any kind of daring. To be naive in this world is an act of daring, and anyone who chooses this form of resistance, hoping thereby to improve his and our world, is extremely courageous. For such a mission, he will have to face malice, which will always seek to challenge ingenuousness, and in the last analysis, he will have to bear playing the fool before the world, so as to avoid wreaking evil in the eyes of God.

And which of us can boast of a healthy diet where ingenuousness is concerned? Who is not attracted by the "concentrated proteins" of opportunism, even if this instills in us huge doses of "cholesterol" of the spirit? The spirit then grows dense, its vitality circulating ever more viscously, until the flow stops. With a congested spirit, we belittle those who are naive, whose life conquests seem to be small.

This is not to argue that martyrdom is a perfect response, nor even that the Holocaust happened because of passive resistance. It is a reading of Singer's artistic call for attention to the absurd reality of Nazi Germany. Nonresistance was not an act of cowardice or an escape from reality. A peaceful people was simply unable to conceptualize or predict to what cruel and despicable lengths the human spirit can go.

Naiveté is usually seen as a handicap, but a better world will not be possible without recovering some measure of it. Give homage to your acts of true ingenuousness. Know how to distinguish them from foolishness and give value to the act of being yourself, before you buy into the package of how most people read reality. Know how to risk and lose in the name of ingenuousness. The lack of ingenuousness is one of the great risk factors that lead to hatred and fighting.

Life Judo

One day, when I was with Rabbi Zalman Schachter-Shalomi in São Paulo, we took a taxi to the airport. Reb Zalman was wearing a big, colorful skullcap covering

most of his head. When we got into the car, Reb Zalman
sat in the front and the driver began sneaking looks at
him out of the corner of his eye. Reb Zalman turned
around and asked me to see if the driver wanted to pose
a question. After I translated, the driver smiled and
went directly to what was on his mind.

"Are you Jewish?"

Reb Zalman understood and said yes. The driver
nodded, as if what he was hearing met with his expectation. But he still kept peeking at Reb Zalman, who
noted the driver's unease and once again turned around
to see if I would inquire whether he had another question.

Once again the driver smiled, happy with a second
opportunity. "Do you all believe in the New Testament?" he asked, leaning toward his door, as if he
feared having touched a nerve. Reb Zalman didn't blink
an eyelash.

"Yes!" he said, to my astonishment, "Yes, but in
our New Testament. We have our own type of New Testament."

The driver reacted immediately, with a smile that
showed he did not totally understand what the rabbi
was saying, but, for some reason, it sounded all right to
him. His body straightened up in the seat, and the initial look of suspicion and curiosity left his face, though
he still drove with a smile on his lips. When we got to
our destination, the driver did not want to charge for the
ride; after much insistence, we paid and got out.

I asked Reb Zalman why he had given that answer

to the taxi driver. He explained, "If I had started to get all involved, saying that we don't believe but that we respect others' beliefs, and if I had sunk into a nice apologetic tone to deal with the estrangement that sparked the question, sitting in a taxi, we would have gotten nowhere. This way, I didn't lie. We have the Talmud, a canonized book that with a little goodwill we can call a New Canonical Text. Instead of dealing with his perception of difference, I used a little 'life judo.' "

What Reb Zalman meant is that with certain questions or situations, we should understand where the other person is coming from at the time he asks the question. Our driver thought the skullcap a very different, strange appurtenance. In inviting him to ask whatever he liked, Reb Zalman wanted to lessen this distance. When the question about the New Testament arose, it came with the violence that makes difference concrete, turning the skullcap into a small monument to how estranged we can feel from others. To deal with this situation, Reb Zalman used the principles of judo, a martial art based on the idea that one should not block a blow, but should move forcefully in the direction of the assault, to neutralize the adversary without the use of a frontal attack.

We see that the taxi driver did not mean to be aggressive, yet his stance would have facilitated a deepening of the estrangement, beginning with his question. Reb Zalman wanted to bring him closer, to be able to explain everything he wanted to, without having to depend exclusively on his verbal message. If he had said no, the driver would have sat differently in his seat, and this posture alone would have made communication even more difficult. Reb Zalman's response actually turned a question that separated and differentiated (which would have appeared totally rude to polite folks), into the best question possible to bring people closer together.

When we know how to act so as to follow the flow of energy coming in our direction, when we don't row against the current, we discover that good, sincere, crude questions can lead to important encounters. Reb Zalman liked the driver because he raised precisely the question that was bothering him, instead of trying to hide it. This indicated that he was open to the idea of moving closer to someone who appeared so strange to him.

Seemingly contrary energy only becomes truly so if we, from the other side, play the role required for this to happen. In life judo, what might appear as an attack to the uninitiated is an incredible opportunity to use the other person's energy, add our own to it, and produce a great deal of movement and life transformation. If we oppose the other person's flow, we create conflict and confrontation, or even cause pain to two bodies that mutually resist each other.

Something similar can be said about human growth. The more direct the energy that questions us, the greater the potential for transformation, if a good life-judo blow is the reaction to it. But if we resist this energy, putting ourselves frontally against it, there will certainly be a great deal of suffering.

We must pay attention and not miss opportunities. When someone says something that raises deep differences of opinion, when blood rushes to the face, indicating that one of our buttons has been pushed, the first impulse should be resisted. This is because we do not want to jump into a mediocre confrontational reaction. For a few micromoments, we should open a window in our soul to the dimension that can greet and welcome the opportunity that is presenting itself.

Just this brief thought, this vague memory that there might be a chance for life judo within our reach— this is all we need to instinctively administer the true blow. After all, when a person comes to us with an issue of difference, might not the true form of opposition be identification? This is the blow of someone who knows how to fight and perceives the true dimension of the conflict. Violence itself does not represent the true area of combat. He who punches well and really wants to hit his opponent should aim at no other target than the heart of all feuding.

6

LIKING THE ENEMY

Rabbi Mikal passed this teaching on to his children: "Pray for your enemies, that all may be well with them. And if you think that this is not serving God, be assured that, more than any kind of prayer, this type of love is truly serving God!"

Strange as it may seem, it may be easier to love an enemy as we would love ourselves than to love a neighbor. The notion of *neighbor* is in fact so abstract that if we replace it with the figure of someone we hate, with whom we have more obvious ties, it becomes much more real and familiar. Our enemies are like family. They permeate our thoughts with the same assiduousness as our friends and acquaintances; we know their lives deeply and we follow them with interest. Thus an enemy is no stranger, and exactly because we hate him, an enemy allows us to create bridges and some familiarity with the concept of "neighbor."

The most distant neighbor ought to be an enemy, but interestingly, the latter ends up being even closer to us than a neighbor. The enemy brings out the idea of "other," but because of his involvement in a person's life, he ends up proving that humanity is one sole body. The farther away, the closer. The Rabbi of Nikolsburg comments:

> It may happen that your own hand inadvertently strikes you. Would you perchance take a stick and attack your own hand in retaliation for your negligence, thus increasing your pain? The same thing occurs when, because of total lack of comprehension in this world, your neighbor, whose soul is one with yours, harms you and causes you to suffer: if you retaliate, you will be the one to suffer.

It is hard to digest the notion that our enemy is part of the same "body" as ours and that hurting him would activate pain in the same nervous system that makes us perceive the pain of his aggression. This is perhaps due to the objective experience that striking an enemy doesn't in the least bring pain to oneself. But if you think this is so, you haven't understood the idea. Let's return to the phrase "Love your neighbor as yourself." Here is the way Rabbi Naḥman of Bratslav saw it:

> What you must do is love your neighbor as you do yourself. There is no one in this world who

knows your many faults and weaknesses as well
as you do! And this does not stand in the way of
loving yourself. In the same way, you should love
your neighbor, no matter how many faults you
find in him.

Maybe this is clearer now: we are all part of one
nature. If we allow ourselves to hate someone else, it is
because we don't know how to sincerely track our own
thoughts and feelings. Hurting an enemy is like attack-
ing one's own hand, since the enemy is identical to us.
And if we were in his place, given the same conditions,
we would be surprised to discover how similar he is
to us. This is why we are all one body—because we
understand humanity as no one else could. If a judicial
court of nonhumans were set up, it would obviously be
inhuman. Thus when it comes to the essence of things,
we are all in the same boat. Hurting this essence in
anyone else, at any time, means hurting ourselves.

Strange as it may seem, liking an enemy is the
path that may lead us to liking our own selves. Thus we
find that this phrase from the future—loving our neighbor as we would ourselves—is, like everything that
comes from the future, totally interactive. There is no
way to like another person without liking oneself, nor of
liking oneself without liking another. This interdepen-
dence originates in the structure of Creation itself.

In the sense of differentiation that arose as part
of the Creation, we came to feel that the perception of
individuality was a greater reality than the perception

of wholeness. But individuality is nothing more than a passing sensation of the incarnate and material. True upliftedness lies in the capacity for understanding all humanity, indeed all life, as part of the same body. Attack another's arm and the pain won't let you sleep.

This is why feuds end in so much regret. Incarnate bodies grow old and start to perceive the transcendental sense of "Hit here, hurt there." Sometimes decades or an entire life goes by before a person feels the blow he struck earlier, but it will hurt him at some point.

Here is the problem of material life: we have enemies. And why do we have enemies? Because we believe we will triumph over them, one day. We create our enmities out of the belief that we are right and that one day justice will bless us. We do not understand that there is no way to win against true enemies, our best enemies. They carry too much of ourselves within them for us to want to see them subjugated and punished.

This is the painful secret: to like an enemy, we must renounce the expectation of winning. And this is very hard. We must at least understand that in its interactive form, beating an enemy means our own defeat, and we will never allow this. Even so, not beating him, we can be fooled into thinking for an entire lifetime that this will occur. For many people, it is only on their deathbeds, as they depart their earthly shells, that the realization dawns that *there are no winners*.

Discover that your best enemy is a savior of many worlds, and you will come to like him. Often, our aversion to an enemy comes precisely from the fact that he opens many doors to internal realities that we are not always ready or willing to face. Liking an enemy is one of the most excruciating tasks in life. We face ourselves with such ferocity that, like Jacob in his struggle with God, our names get mixed up. The personality seems to be on the verge of collapse, and when this happens, a new day is born. One's name has changed.

There are many stories about this kind of struggle. Everyone has had a taste of it, and this is how some rabbis expressed it:

Rabbi David of Lelov said: "I am not worthy of being treated like a just man, because I still feel more love for my own children than for other people."

The Rabbi of Gastinin said: "The Kotsker, my most revered master, strove with great effort to instill in me a love for life, in such a way and with such perfection that I could try to love my enemies with the same intensity as I love my best friends."

Nonhating

To pull back from a feud, it is necessary not only to understand an adversary's human nature, but also to recognize the true magnitude of a misunderstanding. An impartial observer of a violent dispute in traffic will probably be shocked at how imprisoned the players become in the universe of their little incident. From another car, it is possible to see how disproportionate and ridiculous the contenders' attitudes are. But they are unable to escape the whirlpool of hatred. From the moment they enter into conflict, they think that very important things are at stake, such as a better world where injustice and the other guy's uncivilized attitude do not prevail. "What kind of a country is this, what sort of world will I be leaving to my children, if I don't stand up to people like this . . . ?" the involved parties say. Soon, a holy war has begun, challenging human values as well as the future of the country and even the world.

The Rabbi of Ger explained, "We read in the commentaries on Cain and Abel that they fought because both wanted to build a sacred temple to God on their land. Since then, this is the excuse that is given for any sort of bloodshed, war, or hatred. It is always said that the conflict is in the name of a holy cause."

Every time we get involved, even in the most insignificant dispute, we believe our cause is sacred. We do not want to let things pass unchecked, because we are acting in the name of things that are very serious and important. In fact, almost every time this happens, we are acting under the direct and absolute command of a wounded ego. Realizing this means beginning the process of disarmament, of lowering one's guard, and finally of "nonhating." The third phase, known as "sweetening," is the last stage of an effort to tame hatred.

How do we fight hatred? In three stages, the rabbis say: *kabbalah* (reception), *haḥna'ah* (conquest), and *hamtakah* (sweetening). The first and second stages are about the capability to receive the initial impact of an aggressive act and absorb it. The Baal Shem Tov had this to say about the subject:

> We find the phrase, "Who is strong? He who tames his passions" (*Pirkei Avot*). The strong can be thus described: "A guard saw that a thief was preparing to rob a house; he shouted and gestured so that the thief was frightened and fled. Another guard, who heard about this, prepared a trap. When the thief entered his house, he captured him and chained him."
>
> A good man, when assaulted by a bad and violent impulse, frightens it. A just man, when assaulted by the same impulse, tames it, masters it, and redirects it in the service of God.

Learning not to scare off evil and to use it is important, because the potential it carries is too valuable to discard. The impulse must be imprisoned and tamed. Only then can it be sweetened, so that we can learn from the process. Without *hahna'ah*, without the conquest, and only with *kabbalah*, reception, can we even be "good guys," but we will never reach the stage of justice and wisdom. As discussed earlier, the "good guy" does not neutralize hatred; he merely frightens it off, thinking to avoid a conflict. But in allowing the hatred to flee, to stay on the loose, he is doing no one a favor.

Getting involved in an effort to tame rancor, instead of scaring it off, is still not enough to truly neutralize it. When someone tames hatred by countering it with reserves of love, a virtuous life, or the fear that giving in to hatred would put too much at risk, he may actually be contributing to the preservation of hatred. This is because the hatred hasn't been eliminated, only deactivated by burning up reserves of love or of positive experiences.

Thus rancor remains, and like nonbiodegradable trash, it becomes a heavy burden for the individual and for society. "Sweetening" has yet to take place, and this is the responsible attitude of anyone who allows himself to get involved with rancor. Educating oneself to do this is like learning not to dump trash in public places. This means understanding that it is not possible to throw something "out," because there is no "out." Hatred that is discounted without being "sweetened" will certainly end up in an individual's own system. Like undissipated energy, it awaits a moment of tension to be discharged.

Sweetening is what this is all about. In order to do this, a person must be aware of many of the topics discussed earlier. First, there is the need for an awareness that no issue will be abandoned without being *sweetened*. This perception alone is in itself a huge step towards sweetening, when allied with a consciousness about human nature, other people's points of view, and a down-to-earth perception of conflict.

Once we allow ourselves to seek sweetening, this reveals itself to us in multiple forms and possibilities. We thus discover, in the search for sweetness, that human nature reveals other people's points of view,

which in turn open the way for a grounded view of conflict, which itself allows a greater understanding of
human nature. The act of sweetening is totally inter-
linked. Reb Bunam gives a very good example of this,
in speaking of a chess match.

> Reb Bunam wanted to open the window to the
> dimension of sweetening for a man who was very
> stubborn and very weak. So he invited him for a
> game of chess, and right at the start, the rabbi
> made a move that was obviously foolish, without
> letting go of his piece. When the man was just
> about to take advantage of this move, the rabbi
> excused himself and changed his move. Soon, the
> rabbi once again intentionally made a bad move.
> But this time, his partner refused to allow him to
> change. The rabbi responded:
>   "You refuse to excuse two false moves in a
> mere game of chess, and yet you expect the Eter-
> nal One to pardon you, no matter how many trans-
> gressions and mistakes you make in your life?"
>   His partner understood the message.

In the chessboard laboratory, Reb Bunam was able
to bring in the many connecting channels of the sweetening elements. He put a confrontation into perspective
by revealing to the other man his point of view of what
was going on during their interaction. At the same time,
he associated his "faults" with those of his game partner and the human condition itself.

Perhaps the secret of undertaking a successful

sweetening lies in the fact that when we make a sincere move toward another person, we are likely to meet up with the "other," the adversary, halfway. What at first seemed impossible to swallow, so bitter as to paralyze us, turns out to be palatable after all, so long as the other party also participates actively and creates the necessary conditions for "re-seasoning" the relationship. As in a tunnel where each person digs from his or her side, the union of two adversaries is accomplished more rapidly than expected when things happen from heart to heart.

What's Happening in the Other Guy's Belly

Rabbi Moshe of Sassov told his disciples: "It was only when I heard a conversation between two farmers that I came to learn how one should truly love one's neighbor.

"The first one asked, 'Tell me, my friend Ivan, do you like me?'

"The second one answered, 'I like you very much!'

"The first said, 'Do you know, my friend, what makes me suffer?'

"The second said, 'How can I know what causes you suffering?'

"The first said, 'If you don't know what makes me suffer, how can you really like me?'

"Understand then, my sons," the Rabbi of Sassov went on, "that to love, to really like some-

one, means knowing what brings pain to a person
like yourself!"

Without knowing what causes a person discomfort,
suffering, or unpleasantness, it is impossible to love
him. Being aware of this fact brings us closer to others
and allows a fundamental sensibility into the relationship. Only the knowledge of another's pain can prevent
behavior that is improper or insensitive, even when this
occurs in the name of love, worry, or concern. Rabbi
Shimon ben Eleazar said:

> Do not try to pacify your peer in his hour of rage,
> nor seek to comfort him when his loved one lies
> dead before him; do not question him at the time
> of a promise; do not try to see him at the moment
> of his misfortune.   (*Pirkei Avot* 4:23)

Knowing how to respect another person's pain and
his moment means being able to discern when it is time
to calm him, comfort him, counsel him, or proffer solidarity. This is what a Yiddish saying calls "knowing
what's happening in the other guy's belly."

Quite obviously, it is very difficult to know what is
happening in a belly that is totally unconnected to one's
own. If it is famished or full of gases, growling or consti-
pated, this is a mystery revealed only to its owner, unknown to the rest of the world. For this reason, Joshua
ben Perahia, in *Pirkei Avot* (Ethics of the Fathers),
warns, "Judge all men and women favorably."

This is most obvious in the marketplace. When merchandise is being weighed, it is better for a merchant to give a customer the benefit of the doubt than to deal with the possibility that the seller, favored by the scales, might commit theft. This relates to all feuds; we must be ready to find out one day that what was going on in the other guy's belly sheds a completely different light on a situation or on our interactions with him. Thus it is better to run the risk of having favored a customer than of ruining one's reputation.

We have all at one time or another felt hatred for someone and later learned something that changed our original point of view. Many times the information learned is not external, since most people do check their facts before entering into a feud. The information is usually about the other person's *inner* reality, about what is going on in his belly.

Evaluating another person is impossible without knowing what makes him suffer; what limits, frightens, or paralyzes him—and what makes him different from us, what cannot be accessed within the parameters of our own experience. Many couples discover this sad reality when, after vowing reciprocal love, they find that they know little about what causes each other's pain. Repeated disappointment is the result of self-deceptive love interactions such as these. We do unto others as we would like to have done unto ourselves, but this is not enough.

It is important to note that, while we should try to think of others as if they were ourselves, and raise them to the category of a truly close one—a neighbor—we should also respect them as *others*. This is the way of the wise and the just. Others have bellies of their own, and loving these other people presupposes that we legitimize their feelings and sensations, even when these are different from our own. Thus, the ability to perceive, in the idiosyncrasies of one's own belly, a model that authenticates and allows for other people's differences, is crucial. This is the only way to turn others into neighbors, not because they are the same as us, but because just as we ourselves are different from others, this other too, as a different person, can come to be seen as a peer, someone close to us.

Hating Yourself As You Would Hate Others

We return to the phrase "Love your neighbor as yourself," in the interests of decoding it for less abstract and subtle realities. As we saw earlier, this phrase carries with it paradoxes and contradictions. During the rush-hour peak on Monday morning, when we are drowned in the noise of the work week, of commitments and survival issues, this phrase makes little sense. No doubt, it is a phrase that makes sense on Saturday for Jews, on Sunday for Christians, and on Friday for Muslims; for most people, it is also a phrase for special times when we are deeply touched by life or death. But how can this phrase be translated into the unredeemed weekday reality?

The first-century sage Hillel was the first to try to capture the meaning of this phrase in a world (Yetzirah, Formation) where its practical expression might be more palpable and more easily absorbed by humans. In the Talmud, the following story is told:

> A Roman once approached the sage Shammai and said, "I will convert to Judaism if you teach me the entire Torah while I stand on one foot!"
>
> Shammai drove the visitor away with the ruler in his hand.
>
> The man then sought out Hillel and repeated his challenge.
>
> Hillel told him, "Do not do to others what you would not have done to yourself. This is the whole Torah. The rest is commentary. Go and learn!"

What did Hillel do? Here, we must see with the eyes of the sage. With his question, the Roman expresses a wish to enter a world that is obviously much more complex and demanding of time and effort than his ability to stand on one foot. But the challenge, which Shammai perceives as disrespectful, is to be able to take the uninitiated person by the hand and to expose him to the riches of the tradition that he might have sought more directly, had he known of their existence.

In other words, Hillel faced the task of reducing the light, the brightness and intensity, of something that would doubtless blind the challenger. First, as the great

teacher he was, Hillel took advantage of a real situation
to teach his concept. The Roman had just been thrown
out by Shammai and thus could certainly identify with
the idea contained in the "what you would not have
done to you" part of the phrase. Beginning with this
identification, Hillel managed to bring the man into another dimension, one that he could see. His second feat
was that he did not use the phrase "Love your neighbor
as yourself." Although these words express more fully
both the essence of the Torah and the Roman's experience with Shammai, they would have been totally
strange to the challenger. Hillel would then have failed
to create a way to fit contents into an undersized vessel—the entire Torah into an uninitiated person.

What Hillel did was *tzimtzum*, the contraction of a
larger reality into a smaller one without sacrificing the
essence of the larger.

This way, he successfully brought the Torah to the
Roman instead of bringing the Roman to the Torah.
After doing this, by exposing the Roman to something
so close and real to himself, and lending him the eyes
of identification so that he could see, all he had to do
was reveal to him that, in addition, all the rest is commentary. Breathe the full value back into the phrase I
gave you, and you will arrive at the Torah. This is Hillel's recommendation: Go and study!

If the Roman applied himself in his studies, he
would certainly have come to formulate "Love your
neighbor as yourself." But this phrase does not belong

to the world of standing on one foot, of the weekday, of needs and consumption.

Yet Hillel's reduction did not apply to just anyone. Despite Shammai's reaction, the Roman symbolizes someone who is ready to knock on doors, seeking to learn. He may even do this rudely (on one foot), but at least he is aware of this desire and does not give up even in the face of reactions such as that of the sage Shammai.

Theoretically, then, it should be possible to reduce our phrase even more, so as to express an even less subtle world (Asiyyah, Action), identifiable even by someone who, unlike the Roman, seeks nothing. How can we become sensitive to our banal everyday consciousness, in relation to our idealistic phrase?

A new try at reduction comes from Rabbi Shmelke, more than fifteen hundred years after Hillel's era. He said:

> We should understand Hillel's phrase, "What is abominable for you, do not do unto others," in the following manner: "What is abominable in others to you, do not do yourself."

Rabbi Shmelke deals with relating in its most basic form. He does not decode interaction from its abstract side of acceptance, recognition, or sensibility, but instead he looks at the concrete element of strangeness. Do not permit others to find strange or unacceptable in you what you find to be unacceptable in others, because you perceive—and this is the lowest consciousness of this—how abominable it is. Paraphrased, this becomes: "Hate yourself as you would hate others."

Feeling the same rage towards ourselves that we feel towards another person when he or she does something unpleasant (that we also do) is the lowest level of "Love your neighbor as yourself." The first stage for the uninitiated person is to be able to hate himself when cutting off another car in traffic, with the same discharge of hatred he feels when someone else does this to him.

When this is achieved, it is soon possible to stop doing things to others which we would not like to have done to us—and then, perhaps, we begin to touch on loving others as we do ourselves.

The accompanying table relates our phrase to the form it takes in the different environments and realities of the four worlds.

Keeping the Stone Thrown at You

> The Rabbi of Talno came to a city that was part of the sphere of influence of the Rabbi of Rezisztov. The latter's disciples became angry over the violation of their master's "territory." One of them, unable to contain his indignation, threw a stone at the Talnor Rabbi's carriage. The rabbi picked up the stone and said to his friends, "I am going to keep this stone as a symbol of the self-sacrifice and veneration of a loyal disciple." Later, the rabbi placed the stone among his dearest belongings.

WORLD	REALITY	PHRASE
ASIYYAH Action	Material	Hate yourself as you would hate others!
YETZIRAH Formation	Emotional	Do not do to others what you would not have others do to you.
BERIAH Creation	Mental	Love your neighbor as yourself.
ATZILUT Emanation	Spiritual	(Love without need for experience based on individualized identification. World of nondifferentiation) Loving oneself is, by definition, loving another.

The Talnor Rabbi's attitude would surprise anyone who didn't know of his ability to put himself in another person's place. From the cultivation of this practice came his capacity to not hate.

Knowing how to keep this stone is a highly sophisticated exercise. It implies an ability to master violence and turn it into something dead and deactivated, fossilized into a monument to peace. The extreme contrast between the violence with which the stone is thrown and the smile on the lips of the rabbi who picks it up is evidence of the great activities occurring in many worlds, so that we can witness this sequence of events as part of our reality.

Actually, to be able to keep a stone that has been thrown at you, as a symbol of *sweetened* violence, without becoming prey to revenge or pride, is to be able to complete the entire cycle leading to sincere nonhating. This is because such an attitude implies the highest of all tasks: that of transforming a symbol of violence into a positive expression. The Rabbi of Talno, who sees something positive in the disciple's attitude before judging him severely, redirects violence and turns it into a lesson for life. As in life judo, the rabbi saw the stone whizzing by as an expression of passion, and instead of opposing it, he added his own energy to the stone. The rabbi's eyes visualized the pupil's passion, but the monument was erected not to what the rabbi saw but rather to what he transformed. The stone of discord comes to be a symbol of affinity

Here thus is a dimension of stones thrown at us, a dimension that often escapes us but offers us incredible life opportunities. Only those who can see are able to perceive this and make use of them. A childhood story of the Rabbi of Kobrin tells us more:

When the Rabbi of Kobrin was a child, his region suffered a terrible drought, and beggars wandered from city to city, seeking food. A great number of them came to his mother's house, and she prepared the fire to cook for them. Some of the mendicants, impatient with the delay, began to offend the woman with aggressive words, and she became so upset she started to weep. Her small son, the future rabbi, said to his mother, "Why should you let this abuse bother you? Doesn't this help you to help them with a pure heart and carry out a good deed with an almost perfect spirit? If, on the contrary, the poor were praising you or blessing you, your gesture of love would have been less worthy, because there would be the doubt that you might have done this to gain recognition, and not in simple obedience to the commandments of the Eternal One or in the name of His Name!"

Often, the tension and violence we deal with could have their negative sides turned around, so as to represent great conquests and progress. However, on seeing a stone come through your window, do not hate. For if you do, it will have found its mark, whether it hits you physically or not. Realize that although in the material world it is not up to you to decide if the stone will hit you or not, in other worlds you carry great influence on this question. In these other worlds, we have greater control over what comes to bear on us, and we should use it. After all, a person who is hit by a stone and allows it to mark him not only physically, but also emotionally and spiritually, will hurt himself a great deal in this life.

Understanding this helps a great deal on the issue of indignation, where we are easy prey. Our impotence to stop unjustly thrown stones from hitting us is only a contingency of a specific dimension. But the same force that turns a stone into a potential source of pain is also available as a potential antidote, located in one of several worlds. When observed from the point of view of the physical world, none of this makes sense; when seen from the point of view of interacting worlds, this is true, incredibly so.

Between the stone thrown and the stone picked up by the rabbi, many worlds interacted in order to transform that which started as an act of aggression into a feeling of communion and identification. If the violence were greater and the stone had hurt the rabbi, he would have held it in even greater esteem, among his cherished belongings. A backwards world? Perhaps, or maybe it is a world where action and inaction are seen from the perspective of all worlds at once. The perspective of all worlds at once is not evoked by will, wishes, or the aspirations of a human being committed to his individuality. On the contrary, such backwards phenomena are the product of a great deal of transcendence and internal work, which lead to behavior attuned to more subtle worlds. From these places—where one loves one's neighbor as oneself, or where loving oneself is by definition loving another—stimuli emanate that will appear backwards to those tied to the more concrete worlds. Thus the stone, symbol of rigidity in its compacted matter, capable of so much violence, turns into an extremely soft, delicate element. It must be kept as an object that has materialized from the other worlds it traveled through.

Keeping a stone that was thrown at you is like keeping a sample of other worlds. Just as the remnants of meteorites that collided with our planet came from the external universe, stones thrown at us are relics from the internal universe.

The Good Eye

One of the biggest difficulties in disarming a feud is letting go of suspicions about other people. Looks that for some reason cannot be met immediately become the evil eye. And when we pick up on an evil eye coming from someone, any chance of communion and affinity goes right out the window: the other is an *enemy*.

In fact, the evil eye is the most manifest symptom of envy and hatred. The other person sees us not as a neighbor, but from the caricatured viewpoint of a stranger. Everyone has had this kind of experience and fears it instinctively, as if our animal makeup included the practice of exchanging looks before engaging in confrontation. We first seek to destroy with a look—to frighten, cause insecurity, or curse—and then get into a fight. In these looks, the message is clear and well received by the other party; it says, "I don't like you, you are not my kind of person!"

It is interesting to note that the human animal's territory is very often so sophisticated that it can turn into time or an opportunity, rather than just a demarcated space. An important moment, such as a celebration or solemn occasion, can become a battlefield. Thus, at an event such as a wedding or a birth, or the celebration of a professional milestone, adrenaline takes over the bloodstream. This is because when humans realize they have marked out a life territory, they become aloof and insecure about possible invasions.

This is the reason for so many legends, especially medieval ones, about witches who have not been invited to the party. *Witch* is the term used in the medieval world to mean "the other," "the stranger." She is not invited because she is an "other," and in classifying her as such, the host puts himself at the mercy of her gaze. The evil eye, or *ayin ha-ra*, is the gaze of an other who, known or unknown, is not close enough to the host to be on the guest list.

Everyone knows people who are "maybe" candidates for a guest list. These are the people we know who are on the edge of our circle of friends, the ones we fear the most. These are our best candidates for enemies; the ones with whom we engage in envy and evil eyes. Often, they may even come to a party, but they are clearly outside the obvious circle of friends. Earlier, we talked about neighbors stigmatized as "others," who become enemies.

The evil eye does not exist unilaterally, and this is fundamental. It emanates and is perceived, and both the emanator and the perceiver are responsible for it. It will be immediately canceled if one party simply deflects it.

For the rabbis, the only way to deflect or neutralize the evil eye is by way of the *ayin ha-tov*, the good eye. Here is an explanation from the Rabbi of Ger:

We are counseled by the Psalmist to shun evil
and do good [Psalm 34:15] . I would add that, if
you find it difficult to follow this advice, you can
first do good; then evil will automatically move
away from you!

In other words, if we find it difficult to avoid the
evil eye relating to one person, we might change our
strategy and try to send a good eye in his direction.
This means, on a more superficial level, giving another
person the benefit of the doubt, or trying to perceive
the dimension of the following advice from Shimon ben
Azai:

Do not underestimate any person and do not be
disdainful of anything, for there is no human
being who does not have his hour and there is
nothing that does not have its place.

(*Pirkei Avot* 4:3)

We could thus recommend that the good eye be
based on good experiences from the past, when we were
surprised by unexpected gestures of love, or even on
the theoretical certainty that people are not to be caricatured either as witches (the strange) or as fairies (the
familiar). On the other hand, we must realize that the
good eye has to come, in the external world, from great
altruism and goodwill. This means forgetting about the
true sources of discord, sources that lead to phenomena
such as being left off guest lists, or getting the evil eye.
But a more far-reaching and mature formula for sending

the good eye to a person we disagree with was given by the great eighteenth-century sage Reb Pinḥas of Koretz.

It is told that Reb Pinḥas was once sought out by a disciple, a well-meaning fellow. He hoped to establish positive connections with those he disagreed with, while avoiding the grave error of forcing them to accept his version of the world, yet maintaining this for himself. Notice the way this is put into religious language, in the master's answer:

> A person asked Reb Pinḥas, "How can I pray that someone will repent of his ways, when this prayer, if heard in the Heavens, represents a clear interference in that person's free will?"
>
> The rabbi responded, "What is God? The totality of souls. Whatever exists as a whole also exists in part. Thus, in every soul all souls are contained. If I change and grow as an individual, I also contain in myself the person I want to help, and he contains me in him. My personal transformation helps to turn the he-in-me into a better person, and the me-in-him as well. In this way, it is easier for the he-in-he to improve.

The above passage obviously needs several readings. There are innumerable secrets in it, beyond the particularities of the theme at hand. But if we quickly sweep through this hybrid language of spirituality and holography, we find an essential recommendation, the key to conflict resolution: the interactive character of everything, in the world and in all the worlds.

To change an attitude about another person, we must understand that there is an other in us and that we are in the other. If we can work and grow as individuals, not only we will benefit, but the other in us will, too. The view or relationship of the other in us is exalted in such a way that it will certainly reflect onto the us-in-the-other element, enriching it as well. And the final result of this movement is the transformation of the other within the other, or the way we see this other.

Once again, we see that the interior cosmos is highly independent of other people's external behavior. As we dive more deeply into this world, we see the direct interconnections with others, without having to pass through many of the distorted communications channels. Thus we can find more harmony through the internal work of personal growth than through a rational decision or good sense about what is externally just. A rule deriving from this truth might be that one should not seek justice in the external world's court system, regardless of how correct and thoughtful this may be, before trying all the internal routes of personal growth. In this internal court, questions can be resolved with other sorts of lawsuits—not I versus him, but I versus I-in-me, or I-in-him. Who could be better at bringing the litigants together than those who muddy the frontiers of foreignness, of what is *other*?

Perhaps all this is too complex for our time, when the understanding of interactive relations is still embryonic. Ecology, while still rudimentary, is opening the way to this new perception, which will be commonplace in the future. What is done here is reflected there, because all is One.

The rabbis began to perceive this starting with a verse where God commits a "Freudian slip." In Exodus 29:45, in asking for the tabernacle to be built, a portable temple for the Hebrews as they wandered the desert, God reveals, "And they will recognize that I am their God who took them out of the land of Egypt so that I could dwell among them. . . ."

Intrigued, commentators debated a great deal about the impression caused by the verse, that the building of the tabernacle would fulfill a desire or even a necessity of the Divinity—as if the Exodus from Egypt and other celestial plans were to satisfy a schedule not for humans, but for God Himself. Nahmanides (eighteenth century) is categorical about this question:

> Using common and simple sense, we would try to accommodate the language to understand that the building of the tabernacle might have been a need of the earth, but this is not so. It expressed a need of the Heavens!

Actually, this verse reveals the interactive character of everything. We cannot need God, by definition, unless He needs us. This has always been the fundamental idea behind the Kabbalah's mysticism: what happens on Earth influences what happens in the Heavens, and vice-versa. These flows of influence and interference mean that the Other (Heaven for Earth or Earth for Heaven) is an indispensable agent for the transformation of self. We perceive that self-improvement is impossible without the aid of another person, who allows self-evaluation and the search for transformation. Thus, if it were not for the other-in-me, a consciousness of I-in-me would be unlikely, and so forth. Interdependency is the generator of the phenomenon of existence.

But all this that is not yet of our time remains pending, awaiting comprehension in the future. We do not yet have the technology for peace; until a more sophisticated interactive consciousness is developed, it will be hard to evaluate this *he-in-me* and *I-in-him*. We see once again that the phrase "Love your neighbor as yourself" is a message from the future, which with slight changes could be read as "Love the other in your self." The other is I-in-him, and I myself am the he-in-me.

At any rate, for those who can visualize this reality, the act of perfecting a good eye has the same reciprocal character as the evil eye. In other words, instead of trying to look at another person sweetly, to excuse him because of circumstances or the like, sweeten yourself, and the result will be automatic: the good eye.

7

THE TECHNOLOGY
OF PEACE

So far, we have seen how hard it is to maintain a harmonious balance between internal satisfaction and expectations regarding the external world. What we call peace is in fact not so much a state or condition, but more of a common consciousness. Such a consciousness would allow, by way of individual good sense and collective justice, the development of an era of consensus regarding rights and duties. Peace is thus the moment when the limits of what can be justly given and received are crystal-clear to all parties in any interaction. When this becomes a common awareness, people will realize that peace does not depend on the immediate execution of justice, but on justice being fully recognized per se.

In other words, the world can attain peace before being able to put into practice the justice that will one day be part of common sense. This is in itself a process and will create a History of its own. As long as satisfactory levels of integrity are attained in personal interaction, discord for the sake of Heaven will proliferate, in an attempt to give form to this new History. For this to happen, we still need to refine our technology of peace.

Over time, there has been progress: jurisprudence, citizenship, democracy, even ecology. But all these advances function by way of a technology that does not manage to take in the other. It is in this sense that our technology is so archaic and corrupt.

To come to this new technology, we will have to invest in programs governing not the external world, but the internal world. These will be consciousness-raising programs about health, education, disarmament, and domains of authority. These areas are just a beginning; many more must be laid out.

And how can these programs be described?

Health consciousness.　　This will alert us about any form of obesity and greed. All excess should be reported and expressed, via spiritual nausea, fevers, or poisoning, and other symptoms which won't be combated, but which will help to regulate health into equilibrium. Spiritual health will be linked to environmental health, insofar as we preserve our universe. This means being aware that our souls share an interconnected and interdependent world; in the same way there is a relationship between ecological consciousness and the physical body.

Education consciousness.   This will allow us to take a correct measurement. In Hebrew, the word for "lesson" (*shiur;* plural, *shiurim*) is the same as the word for "measure." Learning a lesson is thus learning a measure. The lesson is made up of subject matter, but rarely do we perceive that our education is set up less in terms of the subject matter as a whole than by the measure in which it is administered to us. A shiur, a lesson, should never be more or less than a certain measure, otherwise nothing will be learned. And being aware of this is fundamental to the self-teaching task set out for the soul.

We need to know the size of each step we take, so that in addition to covering a certain distance, we may also learn from its specific size. This is one of the great challenges in the conquest of peace. If we administer to ourselves the wrong shiurim, measures that are either too large or too small for our learning capacity, we put at risk any process of growth or peace.

Educational consciousness is a regulating force, so that we do not alienate ourselves from our capacities or underestimate our limits. Every time our potentials and limits are correctly measured, we complete a lesson. The most impressive part about this process is that, just as the latest measurement is assimilated, our potentials and limits change, so as to accommodate new measurements/lessons.

Disarmament consciousness.   This will help to develop the perception that no peace process can take place as long as we are armed or defensive in relation to others. This is the consciousness of Aaron, the brother of Moses. About him it is said:

> When two men started a conflict, Aaron sought out each one. Sitting down with the first man, he said, "My son, look at what your neighbor is saying! He beats his chest and tears his clothing, crying, 'How can I raise my face and look in the eyes of my companion! I am ashamed, as it was I who did wrong!' " Aaron remained with this person until all the rancor was removed from his heart.
>
> He then sat with the other party to the conflict and said, "My son, look at what your neighbor is saying! He beats his chest and tears his clothing, crying, 'How can I raise my face and look in the eyes of my companion! I am ashamed, as it was I who did wrong!' "
>
> He then remained with this one until all rancor was removed from his heart. And when the two contenders met once again, they embraced and reconciled their differences.
>
> *(Avot de-Rabbi Natan*, chap. 12)

Disarming entails making use of the awareness that we tend to corner a neighbor into playing the role of the *other*. As we come to identify with the other, our vision improves. Identifying is thus seeing. Aaron's mediation teaches us that what is told to both parties does not necessarily have to have truly been expressed. Aaron's "lie" serves to demonstrate that the dimension of possibility, that both might come to express exactly what each was told about the other, is in itself enough to bring them closer and identify with each other.

Aaron is not merely ignoring the details of the dispute; he tries to get around the rancor coming from the world of imagination and fantasy. This is why his method (perhaps the first instance of therapy using visualization) works. He fights image with image. Once the differences created by the imagination are neutralized, the dispute becomes, if not insignificant, at least unable to sustain enmity and feuding.

Disarmament consciousness is about the ability to simulate conditions encouraging encounters with the other.

Consciousness of domains of authority. This consciousness tries to determine the actual authority we have to judge. As we perceive limitations on putting oneself in another person's place and judging him from his own position, we open space for coming closer to others.

There is a story about the priests from a certain medieval town who sought out the king to complain that the tower of the synagogue was higher than that of the church. The king answered, "I govern the breadth and width of the land. For height, there is another Ruler."

The king's wise answer encouraged peace. In recognizing different realms of authority, the king was sensible, refusing to make judgments in areas that were not his domain. This kind of consciousness helps us to decide when we should have an opinion and when we should seek the counsel of other people and institutions.

Peace is a process in which we must abdicate taking the law not only into our own hands, but also into our own hearts and minds. The lover of peace creates an internal auditing process, to supervise the truth of his intentions and the authority he should or should not have to judge others.

Peace through Fear

> Rabbi Yohanan's disciples approached him, saying, "Rabbi, bless us!"
>
> He replied, "May the will of God be that your fear of Him be as great as your fear of men!"
>
> They then asked, "Is that all, rabbi?"
>
> The rabbi responded, "When someone commits a transgression, he secretly says to himself, 'I hope that no one is watching.' He thus shows his fear of men, not of Him!"

We fear the other, in his capacity to bring our behavior and impulses into the realm of existence. Through the eyes of another person, we feel gauged in terms of who we are. When we are caught doing something wrong, we cannot deny to ourselves that we are capable of such behavior. This truth shows how incredibly limited our conscience is, in terms of identity. We know ourselves in great part from what others see of us, in the way their gazes legitimate us. Secretly, we can act in ways that, if observed, would turn us into insomniac worriers preocuppied with blame and fear.

This phenomenon shows how primitive our behavior is when contrasted with our dreams of achieving a more sophisticated technology of peace. Our conscience only produces clear feelings of shame in relation to actions that can be observed by others.

Just as the emotional and spiritual *Homo sapiens*—Adam and Eve—sought to hide their nakedness with fig leaves, we are only concerned with the outer nudity which our conscience makes us perceive. These primeval humans reached a level of wisdom where they recognized the external aspect of the world, and differentiated the real from the imagined. The real was what could be seen and confirmed by others; the imagined was an intimate area, off limits to others. The imagined and the intended were not causes for shame.

We are thus engaged in a search for a new technology of relationship, awaiting an even deeper move into the terrain beyond paradise. We need a new model of a primal couple, one that stresses the shame they feel about what goes on in their minds and spirits, and not just about what is visible externally. This is the dimension where we discover that our intentions possess the same validity as our behavior. Thus our area of responsibility, that which defines us as individuals, widens to include the dimension of intent. As for human nature, our innermost impulses (yetzer ha-ra), are only constrained and regulated by the intent of the intent, as we saw above, and still lie beyond the reach of conscience.

We should understand that the use of concepts such as "widening the reach of shame" may lead to the expression of apparently negative sentiments, such as blame or remorse. But this is using the language of an old paradigm to allude to a new one that is still developing. It is in this spirit that Rabbi Yohanan blesses his disciples, asking them to fear God as much as they do men. Obviously, he does not wish for a world ruled by the tyranny of a God who sees all and thus eliminates any chance for free will. At the same time, his goal is to bring a subtle consciousness down to a lower level, where it can be grasped.

If human beings could visualize God (*le-havdil*, may this example not be taken literally) dressed in a white suit, like the Mafia *padrino* of the greatest of all organizations, with branch offices in all corners of the universe and total aversion to disloyalty, if people could fear Him as they fear what is mundane, then they would be able to raise ever more subtle dimensions to the category of reality. This is because God is not a flesh-and-blood *mafioso* whose punch hurts or whose bullet pierces the skin. To deal with more subtle worlds using the same consciousness we use to deal with the world of matter is to follow up on the original act of tasting the fruit of the Tree of Knowledge. And this is how the process goes: there is no possible return to paradise that does not imply a path through new consciousnesses (or shames, as the old paradigms say); but we will not return through the same gate through which we were expelled. Instead, it will be a gate we did not know existed.

The rabbis visualized this process, where external fear would gradually be replaced by internal fear, or where external shame would be substituted by internal shame. The Riziner Rebbe commented:

> This is why God has waited for our days: because in the days of the Temple we had death penalties and the whip, and there was little space for free will. Later, Israel created severe penal codes, and there was still no free will. But today, everyone can sin openly without shame, they can live and prosper. Thus, anyone who leads a life of integrity possesses great merit in the eyes of the Eternal One, and from this will come salvation!

Nowadays, the image of a punitive God is disappearing; at a time when a new world arises, when it is even an institutionalized practice to go to therapists to eliminate guilt and shame, only in this era can true fear and true shame be salvaged. This new being who can come to exist in times such as ours can see, beyond the nudity of physical reality, to the nudity of the soul. And if, on the one hand, the old paradigm speaks of the conscience manifesting itself in shame, on the other it talks of love and attraction. The nudity the eyes see brings passion to forms and to the body; the nudity that the spirit sees brings new forms of attraction and love of the greatness of spirit.

To demand a world where peace can be attained without *fear* is to believe in a return to paradise, where it is possible to return to the path of expulsion itself. To think this is ingenuous. The true path is that of *fear*, of conscience and of shame. But when we speak of fear, we speak of it within the new paradigm of conscience and shame, one that this generation is beginning to glimpse. Fear of the absolute, of the ever more absolute, is the only way to avoid idolatry, which is to want a peace that is not peace.

Peace attained via lesser fears is illusory and transitory. It is reduced to a goal, when it should be a process. And the process is an unceasing search for new fears, with an ever wider reach. Fears of something and fears for something. Fear that is no other than the greatest fear we can feel for that which is in our interest. Fear for family members, for neighbors, for others, and especially for enemies. The more we fear and the more we fear for, one day we will discover that we fear the same objective that we fear for. On this day, we will have returned to paradise through a new gate.

Peace as a Vessel of Blessing

> You will find no other vessel as safe for a blessing as peace!
>
> —*Berakhot*

Rarely do we realize that a blessing needs a vessel. If we stop to think about what the Talmud tells us, we should first understand that a blessing is a general form of grace that life or the Eternal One (depending on the language we feel most comfortable with) brings us. In order to perceive this grace, we must have special means of keeping it close. This is because a blessing is fluid. Grace in itself can be concrete and real, but its perception—the blessing—is fluid. Many people live in the midst of innumerable graces without realizing they are blessed: "Here is the bread and here is the water—but if there is no peace, there is nothing!" (*Sifra*).

In order to make use of even matter itself, an internal posture of spirit called peace is needed. Without peace, we cannot experience any sort of gratitude and thus we deprive ourselves of a fundamental component of pleasure and well-being. A person without peace has no receptacle to collect blessings and lives with a scarcity of gratitude. This absence is filled with nongratitude—that is, envy. The person who envies is in fact someone who lacks the means to collect the blessings that fall all around him. His envious despair is being able to watch others around him making use of the blessings, without understanding why they are not in his reach, too. What he does not perceive is that his own envy is what prevents him from experiencing his blessings, since envy is "porous" and won't retain the fluidity of a blessing. It is as if, enviously watching a child playing happily with a toy, an observer discovers that in the instant of his distraction, his own toy has disappeared from his hands.

Where did the toy go? Into the hands of the one

who "soaks up the blessings," the one who in his peace symbolizes having something that is ours, that we identify with absolute certainty as ours, something we will fight with all our might to regain. In fact, the envier envies the peace he identifies as his own, as if this is what was stolen away from him. His envy is directed at the other, who does not feel envy. We could thus say that all those who envy are envious of the other's ability to *not envy*. All enviers dream of being able to retain the feeling of gratitude, for which they need the vessel of peace.

This peace is obtained by way of a very tenuous equilibrium, which we seek from infancy onwards. It is an equilibrium between visions and perspectives of the world that a small Hasidic image will help to understand. It is said we have "two pockets":

> Everyone should have two pockets, so that he can go to one or to the other, depending on his needs. In the right pocket should be the words "The world was created for me!" and in the left pocket, "I am dust and to dust I shall return."

Peace comes from the creative ability to keep the pockets straight. Every time we go to the wrong pocket at a moment that demands the other pocket, we open space for envy. If the moment demands the affirmation that we are dust and we go to the one saying that the world was created for us, we come to envy through greed and covetousness. If, on the other hand, we need the pocket saying the world was created for us, and we go to the pocket telling us we are destined to be dust, we come to envy by way of emotional neediness and frustration.

The disaster of mixing up the pockets destroys our state of peace. In one mixup, we seek recognition from an external world that comes back at us with disdain; in another, we lack the self-esteem needed to take what the world offers us. The wrong pockets are about wanting when nothing is offered to us, and about not knowing how to receive when something is put at our disposal. They represent the chaos between internal satisfaction and expectations about the external world, and this is how lack of peace is defined.

We all experience this discordance, in different degrees. Laments such as "I always want something impossible or unattainable," or "If I had only seized that opportunity, my life would be different," are expressions of the daily difficulty we have in getting to the correct pocket.

The most important element in creating conditions for collecting blessings lies in the existential character of each of the pockets. One pocket expresses our euphoria in recognizing ourselves as part of everything, of the marvel of being part of the image and semblance of the One. The other reminds us of the finiteness and the sharing aspect of life, where our individuality will disappear, making the world our inheritor. In both pockets, there are connections between the individual and the whole. The two messages express something similar about recognizing our essence as being part of one Whole. The first is about the world of compassion, and the second about the world of severity. Going to the compassion pocket when we need severity, and vice-versa, is the fastest and most common way to destroy peace, to become disappointed with this world, and gradually to become envious.

Just as the eyes are for seeing and the ears for hearing, peace is for perceiving blessings; it is the "immunological" protection against envy. Without peace, becoming ill is just a question of time.

Causes and Time

> If you live long enough, you will live to see it all.
> —*Yiddish proverb*

Whatever the cause of a feud, it will disappear over time. No matter how grand or important the feud may appear at a particular moment, it will come to emptiness and irrelevance. This knowledge is commonly achieved in old age, on one's deathbed, or in the proximity of a tombstone. If those who know this truth could only reveal it to others efficiently, they would spur great progress in the technology of peace for our times.

They would thus allow us to see that discord that is not for the sake of Heaven has no value and represents a great waste of life. And what are these discords for the sake of Heaven? Those that remain, even after coming under the scrutiny of the triple conscience:

Three things prevent you from committing errors:
know from whence you came, whither you are
going, and before Whom you must account for
yourself!   (*Pirkei Avot* 3:1)

All discord that is truly "sterilized" by means of this
triple conscience—whence, whither, and before
Whom—is discord for the sake of Heaven. This is how
all corporeal and material attachments are eliminated,
to reveal high levels of spiritual purity. When we are
truly conscious of who we are and where we are going,
there is no room for feuds, because they are instantly
turned into dialogue. Such conversations between one
being and another, or between one being and his world,
are only possible once it has been proven that he is not
talking to himself.

Here is the crux of a feud: the belief that we are
intensely interacting with others when in fact we are
totally alone. Many people who think they are very com-
municative and outgoing would be surprised to find out
how lonely their lives are. If they could see from the
perspective of the other worlds, they would see themselves as agitated people, in a big room where they talk,
gesticulate, and rage to themselves. There is no one
else, because there is no room left. They are so full of
themselves, as the Hasidic masters would say, that
there isn't even room for God.

The greater the cause of a person who feuds, or
the more he thinks how indispensable it is to him and
to the world, the more suffocated he will be with him-

self. His only hope, the only way out, is his enemies. These are the ones who can save lives in many worlds, since they can point to the exit from the labyrinthine catacombs where every path takes one back to oneself. By way of an embrace, they can restore the triple conscience: where we come from, where we are going, and to Whom we must make account.

Only time will tell how important our enemies were. We learn, one way or another, the bitter taste of when they are removed to a distant place, or when they pass away and take with them a part of us, a part we will never recapture or know again. "How can you hate me? How can someone not like what I like more than anything else in this world? What did this enemy see in me that is so intriguing to me? How could he not like me?" These are all enigmas that consume lifetimes. Our enemies know something about us that we avoid knowing, by keeping them as enemies. The loss of an enemy is one of the deepest feelings of loneliness and nostalgia, comparable only to the loss of a best friend. To lose an enemy is to meet up again with the conscience of "whither we are going" and how easy it is to allow part of us, together with the one who leaves us behind, to vanish.

Accepting the shadow part of ourselves that can be shown to us through an enemy's perspective is an experience so cruel and enlightening that in itself it would be enough to end all feuds.

The truth is that with time, causes go away and leave us alone. Those who become involved in disputes for the sake of Heaven encounter a reality not at all foreign to them; after all, they always knew where they came from, where they were going, and to Whom they would be accountable. Those who invested time and energy in feuds discover, in later solitude, the emptiness that was their life. They will be forever tormented by the ghosts of what has departed and by the monsters of remorse.

The great cost of feuds through time is the loneliness of realizing that all causes are foolish, of facing the emptiness and randomness of life, with a great deal of painful soul-searching and depression. The loneliness that time unveils, when the greed of youth tires, is a terrible payment to be extracted from old age. It is a loneliness that comes not from the absence of others, but from the inability to find oneself in the midst of so much falsity and wasted life energy. A legend from the Talmud transports us closer to this truth:

> On one of his journeys, by a road, Ḥoni the Circle Maker saw a man planting a carob tree. Ḥoni asked him how long it would take for the tree to give fruit, and heard the answer, "Seventy years."
>
> Ḥoni sat down to eat and felt a dizziness take him over. He lay down and fell asleep. And, as his sleep deepened, stones began to rise up around him and cover him, so that he was not seen by anyone. He went on sleeping for seventy years.
>
> When Ḥoni awoke, he saw a man taking fruit from the carob tree.

"Are you by any chance the man who planted this tree?" asked Ḥoni.

"No, I am his grandson," the man said.

"It is obvious that I have slept for seventy years!" exclaimed Ḥoni in total perplexity.

He then saw that, in the place of his donkey, several generations of donkeys were grazing in the field.

Ḥoni returned to the place where he had lived. "The son of Ḥoni the Circle Maker, is he still alive?" he asked the people from around.

"His son, no," they answered. "But his grandson is still alive."

"I am Ḥoni the Circle Maker," he said. But no one believed him.

Ḥoni left his house and went to the house of study, where he could hear the students debating.

"The law is as obvious to us, as in the days of Ḥoni the Circle Maker," he heard them say. "This is because every time Ḥoni came to the house of study, he was able to clarify any doubt the students had about a text."

"I am Ḥoni," he shouted, euphoric.

But the students did not believe him and didn't give him the attention or respect that Ḥoni had received in the past.

Deeply hurt, Ḥoni asked the Heavens to let him die. His prayers were heard and he died.

Said the sage Rabba, "From this tragedy comes the saying: Either life among friends, or death!"   (*Taanit* 23a)

Ḥoni's nightmare, which inhabits every unconscious, is about the deep perception of our temporality.
During our lives, we develop interactions and discord
for the sake of Heaven, with everyone. We talk with
others by way of identification and the ability to share
in issues common to us. We can do this using the "grav-
itational" escape of our egos. Our common questions,
our difficulties, our pain, and our dreams set up this
link, allowing a meeting with the other.

Ḥoni came up against a world of the future that
was real, where the tree grew and gave fruit as might be
expected; the donkey reproduced; and time, through
the existence of his grandson, showed it had done its
job. But Ḥoni, at the level of honor and respect, could
no longer interact with the inhabitants of this future. All
the small stories had been buried and were decompos-
ing with the world of the past. The envies and feuds that
fed a generation and consumed their time had lost all
meaning.

Ḥoni could have made contact with the world of
the future by way of text, which he knew well. But the
void was so terrible that Ḥoni had no more energy to
pick up on a dialogue with the people of the time he
had come to. We could say the same about people who
sleep through life, for "seventy years."

Ḥoni fell asleep because unconsciously he was enchanted with the image of a man planting a tree whose
fruits would only be harvested seventy years later. His
wish to be present when the fruit blossomed made him

"fall asleep" for seventy years. But his awakening is tragic.

Any one of us who at some moment finds himself enchanted by a magic expectation of the future, who becomes inebriated or seduced by concrete objectives, such as the fruits of a recently planted tree, can enter a state of dormancy.

What we discover in the world of sleep to which we have dedicated ourselves (envy) is that the difficulty in crossing the barrier of one's own "self" is deeply embedded in one's essence. Living with a tree whose fruits are meant for others and for the future is often too much to bear. The child deep within is not so easily convinced by the opportunities for sublimation presented by education and the vision of what is divine inside us. The child is tempted to take from the tree what it has yet to give; he wants it badly, and his polished exterior is not up to the task of limiting fleshly desire. After all, our collective myth is about not having been able to contain ourselves and having taken the fruit from the Tree.

Thus we see that either in Adam and Eve's direct behavior, or in Ḥoni's indirectly expressed need, we all want to go to the fruit of the tree. Those who take this path find out that the guardian of the tree is time itself. Time can bring the fruit to us, just as it took it to Ḥoni. But he discovers that time is both the caretaker of the fruit and the one who charges its high price. Time is part of the Tree of Knowledge and the Tree of Life. He who seeks wisdom needs time to make use of the fruit; this time, however, is life itself.

Our desire to obtain and know, rooted in the expulsion from paradise by the dimension of knowledge and conscience, can only be balanced via a perception of temporality. Knowing where we came from, whither we are going, and to Whom we must make account is the only brake we have on the headlong descent from desire and individuality. Honi's nightmare is finding out that the Tree of Knowledge is a trap, except when tempered by the Tree of Life. The first, alone, renders us obese, unbalanced in the different worlds. Life, time, and mortality are essential to conscience. If not for time and bitter lessons, we would not be able to communicate with one another. We would be prisoners of a world limited to ourselves, where knowledge would not be gauged by life and would have no relevance.

What is important here is what Rabba concluded: it is better to die than live in a world where we are not seen or recognized by others! The envier, defender of small causes, of causes closed into his own egocentric world, is a loner. He does not communicate with others; he says he is so-and-so, and no one believes what he says. He becomes a zombie in a world that lives and exists beyond him—he misses the boat of existence.

The pleasure of this world is in Honi's journey, in the act of Honi sitting down to eat, in watching what the other plants, in the chance to ask and be answered by the other. His dizziness and his sleepiness are a disaster. Perhaps the most frightening aspect of this story is the ease with which processes such as Ḥoni's sleep can come into our lives. What did he do? He simply allowed a marginal image, absolutely incidental in his life, of a tree that takes seventy years to bear fruit, to take over his waking state. This image made him sleep for many, many years, like millions of human beings, who are later shaken awake by illness or tragic life events. Then they ask themselves, perplexed and incredulous, "My God, how did I get here?"

Envy brought them, one by one, to a future where fruit cost a life; a moment of perception that the fruit are not illusory, but our capacity to benefit from them is. Protected by time, the only fruit we are allowed to make use of are those of our own time. The envier does not know this, but the grateful man or woman is fully conscious of it.

Unconditional Love

> Any love that depends on external reasons, when those reasons disappear, the love also disappears; all love that does not depend on external reasons will never vanish.
>
> —*Pirkei Avot* 5:19

Whenever we talk about envy, we are also talking about the question of love. All envy springs from a "short-circuit" of love. Love is fundamental to any technology of peace and even to a better understanding of the phrase "Love your neighbor as yourself."

We have already touched on this many times in the course of this book. But we need a definition of love, to prevent it from becoming a source of misunderstanding. After all, for love we kill, steal, and envy—even victimizing the object of our love. For love we go to war, become obsessed, or block the paths to knowledge.

Even the love we feel for ourselves may actually depend on external reasons. Once these reasons cease to exist, our love for ourselves will also die. How many times have power, fame, and ambition left people to wander through life, once the reason for their self-love is gone? This is why legions of well-meaning people have gone out to try to love their neighbors, but few have returned. Each one was gradually swallowed up by "reasons" to love, and was corrupted.

Anyone who dares to defy his animal dimension and take on the task of loving without cause, incorporating this form of love into his very nature, betrays his own humanity. His arrogance will be erased at the first real chance to love someone without external reasons, because he will surely fail. We looked at the cause of this failure earlier, when discussing the "intention of the intention," the yetzer ha-ra, or evil (animal) inclination. Thus, when a person blocks his animal impulse, he will not only fail at his objective, but he will also suffer deeply. We are not Divinity, but merely its image and semblance.

Then is there no love without external reasons in human experience? Yes, but it must not be confused with an idealization, a utopia not yet possible. What would this love without external reasons be, then? It would be the love of intention, not of the "intention of the intention." It would be a love originating from the spontaneity of nonanimal intent. Perhaps we can understand this better with a story from the Midrash, about the verse which says: "If you see the ass of the one you hate stretched out on the ground because of its burden, you will not pass by, but you will liberate the ass and its owner" (Exodus 23:5). The Midrash says:

> Rabbi Alexandri shared the event that occurred: Two men who hated each other passed with their asses on the same road. The ass belonging to one of them fell with its heavy load and his adversary passed by. But suddenly, this one said to himself, "It is written in the Torah that one should not pass by the ass of an enemy, when he is in difficulty." He then, without thinking for even an instant more, turned around and helped to load the ass again. The owner of the ass began to think in his heart, "This man is really my friend and I did not know it!" The two then went on together in the direction of a tavern and they ate and drank at the same table.

The importance of this story is that spontaneity mediated the chance for these two men to meet. The first impulse of the man whose ass was perfectly fine was to walk around the fallen one. But his spontaneity (and there is no reason to suspect his sincerity) arose from his ability to mediate between his learning and the situation. We should perceive that it is an act of subliminal love which allows the memory to bring forth the verse in question. If he had wanted to forget the meaning of the verse, he could have easily done so, since the intellect is capable of great and convincing articulations of this nature.

What makes the man return to help his companion is a love that has no external reason. In his heart, in the junction of his individual self with his tradition, it was possible for this man to express a generic love to the world and its Creator, a love which found in the other, the one who needed help, an agent. The fact that this was his enemy was irrelevant, as it would be if he were the man's best friend.

We can thus understand how it is possible to make contact with another person, through love. First, an intermediate, generic love is necessary, one we believe in and value in ourselves as divine image and semblance. This gratuitous love for others is the kind that needs no external reason, but depends on the underpinnings of a tradition, knowledge, and even of the law.

This is why a person who goes out with the intention of loving another person as he loves himself, without the elements of this generic love associated with a moral code and knowledge, will fail.

We must be very careful not to confuse this process with the nonhuman capacity to simply love another person without mediation. Without turning the other into someone like ourselves, we cannot love him or her. Without coming into contact with our spiritual world, which recaptures the interactive dimension of everyone and everything, there is no mediation.

The evolution of life leads us to understand that love is not a condition of the past, but of the future. As on Monday, the second day of Creation, difference established discord and dispute; on Tuesday, a slow and gradual process began among those who are different, as they began to recognize each other. And from this recognition of the "one" within the "other," growth is made possible for both human conscience and life.

Envy in the World to Come

In the world to come, we will all be studying with our enemies. They will be our partners, and in twosomes (*hevrutas*), we will review one by one our acts of envy and hatred. We will not do this in any court, as we imagined on Earth. Good and evil will be subjects for study, and not for punishment or recompense, the way our obsolete conscience conceptualizes; after all, as the rabbis say, in empty space there is no right or left.

On Earth, we cannot understand what it means to lose one's individuality, to cease being differentiated. We cannot imagine exchange and interaction without having a subject, a vessel, and that is why we still speculate on future punishment and recompense. But these are perceptions of the material dimension, where depressed and euphoric people are at the mercy of caprice.

The world to come holds many surprises, especially regarding envy. To get a glimpse of the waiting room of this world we should allow ourselves to understand a bit more of its ambiance. Here is how a Hasidic commentary described it:

> In the Scriptures, we read (Deuteronomy 5:5): "I put myself between all of you and God." The "I" is between God and us. But there are no barriers separating or dividing one who sacrifices his "I." About this, the Song of Songs says, "I belong to my beloved and he belongs to me." When my "I" come to belong to my beloved, "he" will come to be mine.

As long as the "I" puts itself between us, the other, and the world, we will not even know the taste of the world to come. Thus, we must know how to bear giving over our "I" to the greatest number of representatives of this "beloved," whether in the form of lover, friend, companion, neighbor, other, or even enemy.

Reb Naḥman of Bratslav said one can only hate or only envy when feeling sad. According to him, the world to come allows the "I" to be given over because it is the world of happiness. Everyone who in this world can find happiness will abandon envy and sink into gratitude. His favorite image was that of a marriage.

Reb Naḥman would imagine himself on the day of his daughter's wedding, at the moment when his most precious jewel is shining with happiness, when life softly caresses his face with a smile that does not disappear. Dancing, guided by the sweet rhythm of the wine, you see everyone in the room, your whole world, spinning around. You climb on the table, and while the lights twinkle in your tears, you dance. If suddenly, your greatest enemy entered the party, what do you think your reaction would be? You would embrace him and he would say the sweetest words to you, leaving your heart light as a feather.

If we could walk the streets, go to work, or be with our family with the state of mind of a daughter's wedding, our enemies would become guests in our lives; envy would turn into a toast to the other: "May your daughter marry soon, and may I be your guest!"

Giving over your "I" is being able to recognize it in the other, creating an openness towards seeing the I-in-him. It is finding out how many hes-in-me exist that can make this world a little more like the one to come. It is turning this life into a big wedding party, where anyone who comes in the door in the middle of our dance becomes a guest. It's a party where there are no witches or evil eyes, because everyone—that is, the *other*—is a guest. Leaving no one out, we lose our fear . . . on this day, at this moment

> They shall beat their swords into plowshares
> and their spears into pruninghooks;
> nation shall not lift up sword against nation,
> neither shall they learn war anymore.
>
> *(Isaiah 2:4)*

But they shall sit, each person under his grapevine and his fig tree, and no one will be afraid anymore.

May this book be a vehicle to honor and give life to the words of the Torah, by the path paved with the lives of those who received it and passed it on.

———————

Completed on the twenty-seventh day of Adar 5752,
when we read in the Scriptures
Moses' invitation to build a sanctuary:
"Tell the children of Israel to bring Me offerings:
from every person who gives it willingly with the heart
you shall take My offering!"
(Exodus 35:5)

References

Buber, Martin. *Ten Rungs*. New York: Schocken Books, 1947.

Bulka, Reuven. *As a Tree by the Waters*. Jerusalem: Feldheim Publishers, 1980.

Chavel, R. Charles. *Between Man and His Fellow Man*. New York: Shilo Publishing House, 1980.

Cohen, Arthur A., and Paul R. Mendes-Flohr. *Contemporary Jewish Religious Thought*. New York: Free Press, 1990.

Disho, David. *Tarbut ha-Maḥloket be-Yisrael*. Tel Aviv: Schocken Books, 1984.

Feinsilver, Alexander. *Talmud for Today*. New York: St. Martin's Press, 1980.

Goldin, Hyman. *Ethics of the Fathers* [*Pirkei Avot*]. New York: Hebrew Publishing Company, 1962.

Kaplan, Aryeh. *Gems of Rabbi Nachman*. Jerusalem: Yeshiva Chassidei Breslov, 1974.

———. *Waters of Eden*. New York: Orthodox Union, 1984.

Kederman, Deborah. *Invisible Chariot*. Denver: Alternatives in Religious Education, 1986.

Klagsbrun, Francine. *Voices of Wisdom*. New York: Pantheon, 1980.

REFERENCES

Klein, Melanie. *Envy and Gratitude and Other Works, 1946–1963*. New York: Free Press, 1975, 1984.

Krohn, R. Pessach. *Maggid Speaks*. New York: ArtScroll, 1987.

Kushner, Lawrence. *Honey from the Rock*. Woodstock, N.Y.: Jewish Lights Publishing, 1990.

Leibowitz, Nehama. *Studies in the Bible*. Jerusalem: Ahva Press, 1980.

Lipman, Eugene. *Mishna*. New York: Norton and Company, 1970.

Loewe, Herbert Martin, and Claude Joseph Montefiore. *Rabbinic Anthology*. Philadelphia: Jewish Publication Society, 1988.

Nachman of Bratslav, Rabbi. *Garden of the Souls*. New York: Breslov Research Institute, 1990.

Newman, Louis. *Hassidic Anthology*. New York: Schocken Books, 1963.

Schwartz, Richard. *Judaism and Global Survival*. New York: Atara Publishing, 1987.

Tsion, Ben Raphael. *Anthology of Jewish Mysticism*. New York: Judaica Press, 1981.

Zalman of Liadi, Rabbi Schneur. *Likutei Maamarei Tania*. New York: Kehot Publishing, 1984.